A SKETCH OF ASSAM

First published 1847
This edition published by Lector House in 2024

ISBN: 978-93-6138-392-2

Lector House LLP
Registered Office: H. No. 96, Block C, Tomar Colony,
Burari, Delhi – 110084, India
info@lectorhouse.com
www.lectorhouse.com

A SKETCH OF ASSAM

MAJOR JOHN BUTLER

2024

LECTOR HOUSE LLP

Garrow warrior.

A SKETCH OF ASSAM:

WITH SOME ACCOUNT OF THE HILL TRIBES.

BY AN OFFICER

IN THE HON. EAST INDIA COMPANY'S
BENGAL NATIVE INFANTRY IN CIVIL EMPLOY.

WITH ILLUSTRATIONS FROM SKETCHES BY THE AUTHOR.

TO

MY FATHER,

WHOSE EARLY TUITION, URBANITY, LEARNING, AND EXAMPLE, ENCOURAGED ME AT THE COMMENCEMENT OF LIFE TO RELY ON MY OWN EXERTIONS, THESE WANDERINGS AND REFLECTIONS IN A WILD, UNCIVILIZED, FOREIGN LAND,

Are Dedicated

WITH THE GREATEST VENERATION,
BY HIS AFFECTIONATE SON.

PREFACE.

To those accustomed only to the comforts of civilized life, or to the traveller who is indifferent to the beauties of scenery, the monotony, silence, and loneliness of the vast forests of Assam, will present few features of attraction; but as the country offers a wide field of discovery, and so many interesting enquiries remain to be prosecuted in regard to the numerous wild tribes by which it is inhabited, it is hoped that the present brief outline of the condition of the people will not prove altogether uninteresting.

The chief object of the following pages is to make Assam better known, to remove some prejudices which exist against it, and preserve the memory of many remarkable scenes. The narrative of the principal events has been compiled from official documents, with the knowledge of Government; but the Author has expressed his own unbiassed opinions on many interesting subjects with which he became acquainted during a residence of some years in the Province. Much more might have been described, but the few authenticated facts now put forth will probably suffice, from their novelty and interest, to amuse the reader until greater leisure and further experience enable the Author to present a more comprehensive work.

CONTENTS

Page

CHAPTER I.

CHAPTER II.

CHAPTER III.

SOME ACCOUNT OF THE ASSAMESE TRIBES.

KHAMTEES.

SINGPHOOS.

MUTTUCKS.

BOR ABORS, ABORS AND MEREES.

MISHMEES.

DOOANEAHS.

ASSAMESE.

NAGAS.

GARROWS.

COSSEAHS.

BOOTEAHS.

SATH BOOTEAH RAJAHS OF KOOREAHPARAH DOOAH, IN DURRUNG.

CHAR DOOAR, OR SHEERGAWN AND ROOPRAE BOOTEAH SATH RAJAHS.

THEBINGEAH BOOTEAHS.

HUZAREE KHAWA AKHAS.

KUPPAH CHOOR AKHAS.

DUFFLAHS.

LIST OF ILLUSTRATIONS

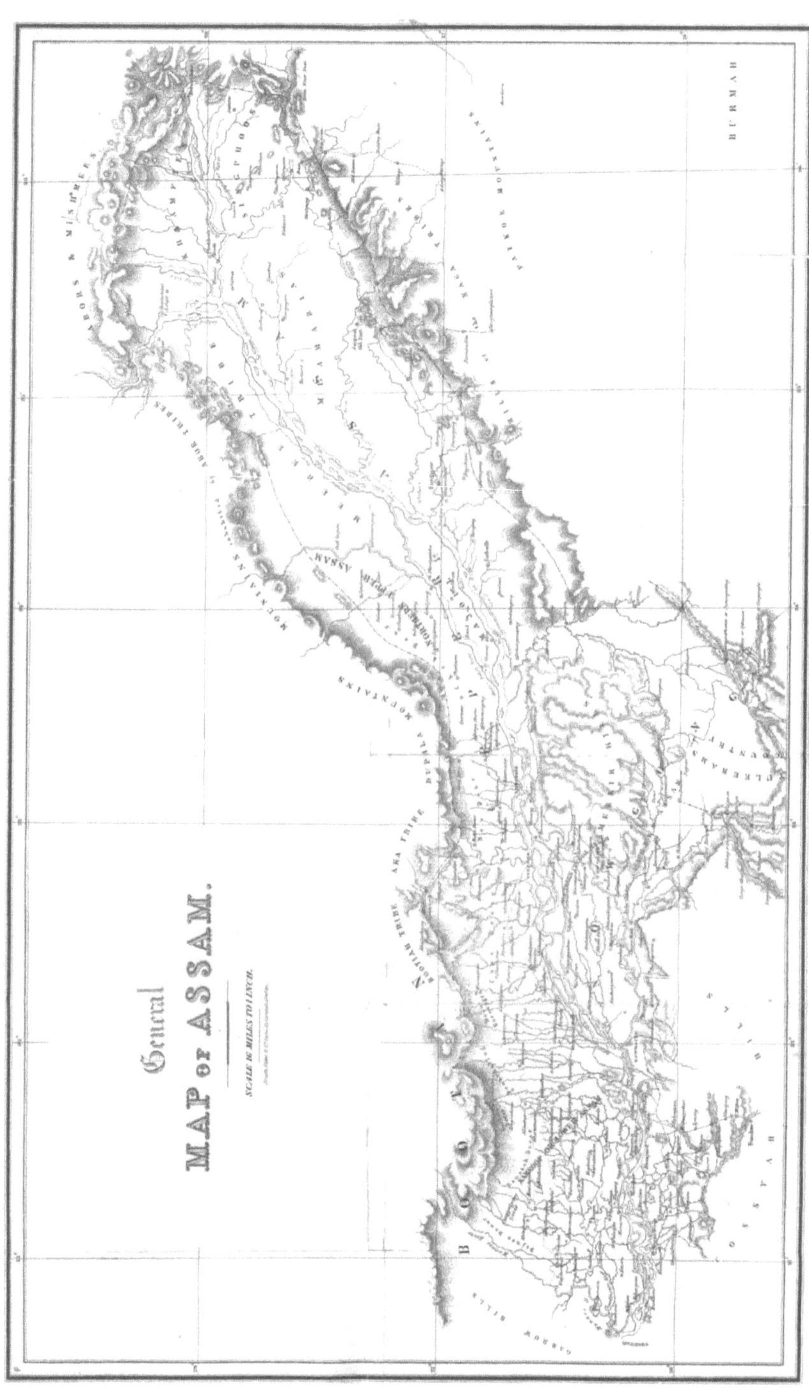

General Map of Assam.

Scale 16 miles to 1 inch.

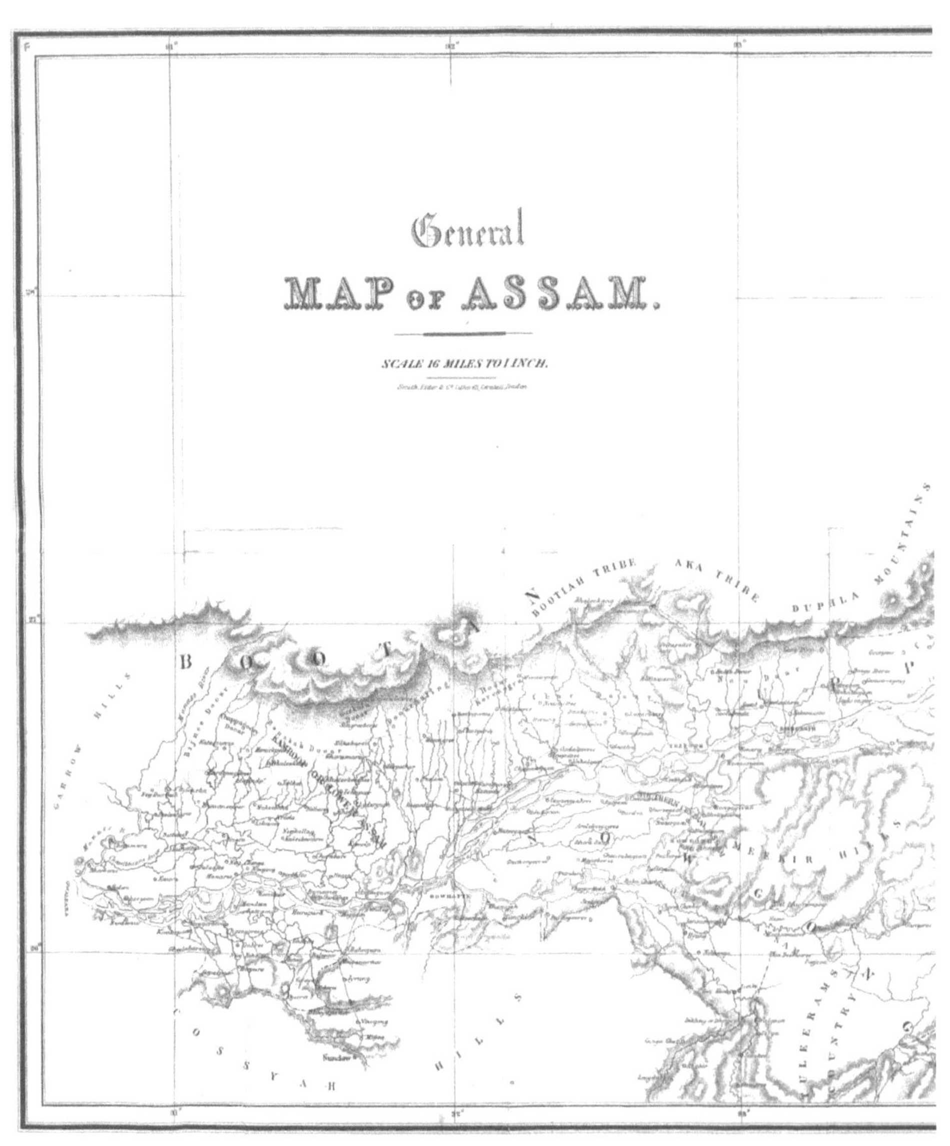

General Map of Assam. (Enlarged - Left)

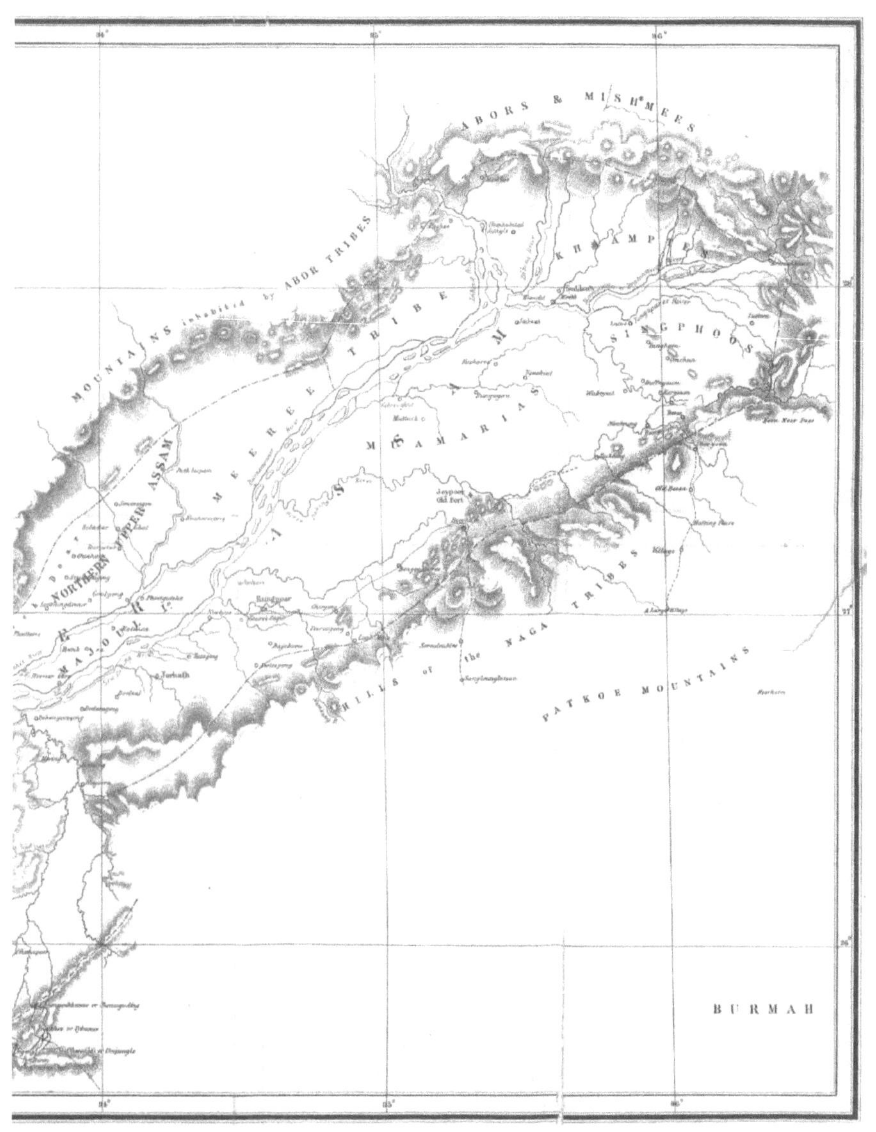

General Map of Assam. (Enlarged - Right)

CHAPTER I.

Appointed second in command of the Assam Light Infantry.—Journey to Assam, Goalparah, and Gowahatty.—Trip to Seebsaugur in a Canoe.—Boats and Dangers.—Seebsaugur and Saikwah described.—The Tribes.—An Assam Cottage.—Unwelcome Intruder.—Climate of Assam.

In November, 1840, being then on duty at Mynpooree in Upper India, with my regiment, in which I filled the office of Interpreter and Quarter-Master, I had the honour of receiving from the Governor-General of India the appointment of second in command to the Assam Light Infantry. Regimental duty amongst our earliest military companions has its charms, but there is not an officer in the East India Company's service, be his attachment to his comrades and the sepoys under him ever so strong, who does not hail with joy the day that gives him comparative freedom, especially when that freedom is accompanied by the proud emotions ever attendant upon the possession of higher command. Accordingly I was much elated at the distinction that had been conferred on me; nor were my pleasurable sensations diminished by the circumstance of the future scenes of my service lying in a country that I had already once visited, and regarding which I felt an uncommon degree of interest. Bidding my friends farewell, therefore, I quitted Mynpooree, marched to Futtyghur, and thence embarking in a native boat upon the Ganges, proceeded to Dacca by the ordinary route, reaching the station in the latter end of December 1840. At Dacca, engaging new and more commodious boats, I again set out on my journey to Assam, and entered the Burrampooter river near the military station of Jumalpore, and arrived at Goalparah, the entrance to Assam, in nineteen days.

The military station of Goalparah is situated on the left bank of the Burrampooter, on the summit of an oblong hill three hundred feet high, commanding one of the most magnificent views of the Bootan and Himalaya Mountains, partially covered with snow, that can well be imagined. There are (or were at the time of which I write) three bungalows (ground floor cottages) on the small space of table land on the hill, occupied by the officers attached to the district. From its elevation, many are disposed to claim for the hill the enviable title of "the Sanitarium of Assam," but however just its pretension to salubrity may be, the same degree of credit cannot be extended beyond this isolated spot. Many parts of the division are so inimical to life, that the mortality both of Europeans and natives, equals, if it does not exceed, that in any district in Assam. The noxious exhalations from the Garrow hills and woods seem more deadly than the climate of the Northern

Dooars, of which few persons resident there can long resist the depressing effects. Unless endowed with great stamina, life is here frequently extinguished by jungle fever in the course of a few days.

The town of Goalparah, consisting of about seven thousand inhabitants, is built wholly of mats, grass, bamboos, and reeds, at the foot of the hills, and as the adjoining country is a low, swampy level, interspersed with slight elevations, it is subject to annual inundations. The chief traders are Kyahs, merchants from the western parts of India; and at no place in Assam is there a more extensive and lucrative trade carried on in cloths of English and Indian manufacture; rice, mustard-seed, cotton from the Garrow hills, manjeet, and other articles.

A three months' residence at the station of Goalparah in 1837, rendered a prolonged stay unnecessary on the present visit. An absence of three years had produced few changes in the condition of the people or the appearance of the buildings, excepting in the house I formerly occupied, which had been suffered to become a heap of ruins. One vestige of the *débris*, however, gratified my self-love. A little glass window-frame, made with my own hands, still survived the destruction of time and the elements, and vividly recalled to memory the difficulty I had overcome in endeavouring to admit light into my little dwelling. Such a luxury as window glass being unknown at the remote station, I had purchased some of the small looking-glasses which always abound in the Indian bazaars, and, removing the quicksilver, converted them into window panes.

Leaving Goalparah, six days were occupied in reaching Gowahatty by water. In Gowahatty, the metropolis of Assam, I perceived a vast change; many buildings of brick had been erected and the foundation of a church laid; numerous native shops evinced increasing prosperity, and much had been accomplished towards rendering the station more salubrious by the removal of jungle and the construction of many beautiful roads. The best and largest bungalows at Gowahatty are all on the banks of the Burrampooter, and the view of the river, the islands, temples, and verdant foliage of the trees forms perhaps one of the most picturesque scenes to be met with in India.

The native town of Gowahatty is built entirely of bamboos, reeds, and grass. To the south an extensive marsh almost surrounds the whole station, and the contiguity of many old tanks, choked with jungle, coupled with the vicinity of the hills on every quarter except the north, renders this town, in spite of the improvements already alluded to, one of the most insalubrious in Assam. In the cold season, from the 1st of November to the 1st of February, the fogs at Gowahatty are extremely dense and heavy, and last frequently until ten or eleven o'clock in the day; but it is generally admitted that this state of the atmosphere is by no means unfavourable to health. The rainy months of June, July, August, and September, are here always trying to Europeans, as the moist heat has a much more depressing influence than the rains of the Western Provinces of India.

View of Gowahatty.

Omanund Island Opposite Gowahatty

Nearly two months having been passed in boats on the river, from Futtyghur to Gowahatty, I became anxious to reach the end of my journey by a more expeditious mode than that of tracking up against the stream a few miles every day. I accordingly quitted my budgerow and embarked in a canoe formed of a single tree hollowed out. It was forty-eight feet long, and three feet wide, ten feet of the length being covered in with a small mat roof, as an apology for a cabin. In this I felt by no means uncomfortable, though I had only a little more room than served to enable me to lie down at full length.

The solitariness of my position, only enlivened by the song of eighteen merry paddlers, pulling from morning till night, at the rate of forty or fifty miles a day, against a rapid stream, was perhaps the worst part of the story. The scenery, if not positively devoid of picturesque beauty, wearied me from its monotonous character. Sand-banks, woods, and hills, unvaried by the residence of man, or the slightest token of civilization, constituted its leading features. Occasionally a boat might be encountered, but, excepting from the rude salutation of the wild crew, the screaming of wild fowl, and the loud crash of falling banks, prostrating lofty trees in the bosom of the river, not a sound was heard to relieve the pervading solitude. But, altogether, the velocity of the trip, with the *désagrément* of limited accommodation, was a good exchange for the comforts of a budgerow, and the tediousness of its pace.

Passing the healthy and pretty stations of Tezpore and Bishnath, I arrived at the mouth of the little stream Dikhoo, in nine days, and, mounting an elephant, rode through a dense tree and grass jungle to Seebsaugur, distant twelve miles from the Burrampooter. It was a bitterly raw, cold, wet day; but a blazing fire on the floor in the snug reed and grass cottage of an acquaintance, soon erased from my memory the inconvenience of the previous ten days' exposure.

In the rains, the Burrampooter river resembles a sea, extending for many miles over the country. In the dry season it will be found in many places more than a mile wide. The current in Upper Assam, above Dibroo Ghur, is much more rapid than the Ganges river, and far more dangerous; from the river being strewed with immense trees, which are whirled down the stream with awful impetuosity, threatening instant destruction to the boat so unfortunate as to come in contact with them. For this reason, the canoes of the country being more manageable, and even if filled with water, too buoyant to sink, much less risk is incurred by travelling in them than in the comfortable budgerow, or large native boat of Western India, roofed with straw. The canoe has also another advantage, in case of a storm, as it can in a few minutes be dragged on shore and remain in perfect safety till the *toofan* has passed over. The confinement, however, and constant reclining posture are almost unbearable in the hot weather; and there is a painful sense of insecurity from the streams and rivers in many parts of Assam swarming with crocodiles. Natives, when bathing, are not unfrequently seized by crocodiles, and I have heard that one of these amphibious monsters has been known to seize a paddler unsuspiciously sleeping in the front part of the boat: which is not improbable, as the sides of a canoe are only six inches or a foot above the water. Such occurrences, however, are too rare to justify the fears that are entertained; but their rarity, considering the great numbers of crocodiles on the banks, is nevertheless a marvel. In the Chawlkhawa river, opposite Burpetah, I have seen basking in the sun on the sand banks, as many as ten crocodiles at a time; and upon one occasion, a heap of one hundred crocodile's eggs, each about the size of a turkey's egg, were discovered on a sand bank, and brought to me; I found on blowing them, that they all contained a perfectly formed crocodile, about two inches long, which would have crept forth after a few days' farther exposure to the sun.

The flesh of the crocodile is like that of fish, emitting the same odour, and partaking of the flavour of the coarsest of the finny tribe. After skinning a small crocodile caught by a fisherman in his net, one of my native servants made a curry of the flesh, which is consumed by some low caste men in Assam, as well as in Western India. The eggs of crocodiles and river turtle are esteemed delicacies. Upon the merits of the flesh of the turtle I need not expatiate. I have frequently endeavoured to shoot the crocodile, but if they be not almost invulnerable, they contrive to elude capture; for when wounded they manage to get into the river, and either escape to recover, or die out of sight. It never was my fortune to kill and secure more than one, which was upwards of twelve feet in length. He was mortally stricken with one ball.

The station of Seebsaugur merits little notice. It is a low, flat country, subject to inundations. There are several large artificial tanks, and one or two fine old Hindoo temples, in and about the station. The fort of Rungpore, built of brick on the opposite side of the Dikhoo stream, is quite in ruins; and of the old city of Rungpore, not a hut is now in existence: all the inhabitants being now apparently located at Seebsaugur, which, from having become the residence of the civil officers in charge of the district, will in a few years, in all probability, be a populous, thriving town. After a few days' residence at Seebsaugur, I again set out in a small boat on the Burrampooter; passing the new station of Dibroo Ghur, the residence of the Political Agent of Upper Assam, and other gentlemen connected with the manufacture of tea, I ascended the dangerous rapid formed by a ridge of stones extending almost across the river, a little below the junction of the two rivers, Dihong and Dibong, with the Burrampooter, and in seven days from Seebsaugur, arrived at the end of my journey, Saikwah. Here I assumed the command of three hundred men, and two six-pounders.

The site of Saikwah, the north-eastern frontier military post in Upper Assam, is on the south bank of the Burrampooter; on low ground, intersected by numerous streams and surrounded with dense high tree-jungle, having the Bisnacorie and the Saikwah streams on the west and east, and the Burrampooter on the north. For the comfort of the troops, a space of about one thousand square yards has been cleared of jungle. In the vicinity of, or a few miles distant from Saikwah, there are some small villages inhabited by tribes denominated Dooaneahs, Moolooks, Kesungs, Jillys, Mishmees, and Meerees who, from their wild habits, prefer the jungles to the plains. They grow a scanty supply of rice, kullie (a species of vetch) and Indian corn; the whole of which is generally consumed in a few months, leaving them to depend for the remainder of the year on leaves of the forest kutchoos (a kind of arrow-root) and wild yams. Saikwah was selected as a military post in

1839, immediately after the station of Suddeah on the opposite or north bank had been surprised and burnt by the neighbouring tribes. It is eighty miles distant from the Patkoe mountains, separating Assam from Burmah; but it is by no means so desirable a station for the health of the troops as the deserted post of Suddeah, in an open plain of six miles in extent. The object, however, of the change of locality, was to enable the Light Infantry to afford protection to the tea-gardens in Muttuck from the sudden aggressions of the numerous wild, fierce, border tribes. In this respect it has answered; hitherto, few depredations having been committed, though insurrections have been frequent.

The trade of Saikwah consists of ivory, wax, and a little cotton; the amount of ivory sold in the bazaar, the shopkeepers informed me, averaged annually about six hundred pounds. A more desolate place than Saikwah can scarcely be imagined. It is surrounded by fierce and treacherous tribes, who occupy a most impenetrable tree and grass jungle, and whose endeavours are perpetually directed to the annihilation of the troops. At first, the hourly patrol's grand rounds and alarms allowed me little rest or ease, but the alertness of the troops in getting under arms at night to repel any meditated attack, soon obliterated from my mind all apprehension of surprise. The Assam Light Infantry wish for nothing better than an opportunity of contending with the Singphoos, or indeed with any of their treacherous neighbours (whom they hold in the utmost contempt) in a fair battle in the open country; but in the jungles they find it almost impossible to come in contact with their foes.

A few days after my arrival at Saikwah sufficed to plaster my mat-and-grass cottage with mud, and with the assistance of the Sipahees, a chimney for a fireplace was soon constructed, with bricks and mortar obtained from old buildings at Suddeah; then putting in a glass window, I was enabled, in comfort and solitariness, to pursue my usual vocations in all weathers. In this secluded retreat, every incident, however trifling in itself, acquired an importance which induced me to note it in my tablets. On one occasion, about eight o'clock at night, sitting by a snug fireside, my attention was arrested by the approach of an unwelcome visitor making his way in at the door. Taking up a candle to ascertain who or what was forcing ingress to my dwelling, I beheld a python, or boa-constrictor, about six feet long, steadily advancing towards me. In my defenceless position it may be imagined that safety depended on immediate flight; and the monster thus speedily gained entire possession of my habitation. It was, however, for a few minutes only, that he was permitted to remain the undisturbed occupant of the abode; for my servants quickly despatched the intruder with a few blows inflicted with long poles. An apothecary, who had long been attached to the Assam Light Infantry, assured me that pythons, or boa-constrictors, were very numerous in our vicinity, and of an immense size, some not being less than fifteen or eighteen feet in length. I had evidence of the truth of the statement; a skin, fifteen feet long, being subsequently brought me by the natives. I caused it to be tanned and sent to England. Small serpents were often met with. On one occasion the apothecary brought me two boa-constrictors of about four feet long, which he had found on a table curled up amongst some bottles in the same room where his children were sleeping. In all probability the lives of the infants were saved by the musquitto curtains preventing access to the bed. Boa-constrictors are exceedingly fond of rats, and on this occasion they had evidently been in search of their prey.

As my cottage had not the usual white cloth ceiling suspended, insects, snakes, and vermin frequently descended from the roof into the rooms; but by keeping the house free of baggage and well swept, contact with them was avoided. The reader will suppose an Assam mat-hut to be a dreary kind of residence; but I can assure him, the logwood fire on a hearth one foot high, in the centre of the room, with a small window cut high in the wall for the escape of the smoke, is by no means devoid of cheerfulness.

The general characteristic of the climate of Upper Assam is excessive moisture. Rains fall heavily and frequently in March, April, and May, and continue to the middle of October; and from this time till February the atmosphere is cool and pleasant. As the bordering hills of Assam, both on the north and south, are peopled by a variety of tribes differing from one another in aspect, language, and customs, I have, in later pages, briefly depicted each class; mingling personal description with a narrative of as much of their respective histories as circumstances have put it in my power to offer.

TABLE.	
Showing the number of days required for a Budgerow to proceed from Calcutta to Suddeah, or Saikwah in Upper Assam, from October till 1st June:—	
	No. of days.
From Calcutta to Dacca	12
From Dacca to Goalparah	19
From Goalparah to Gowahatty	6
From Gowahatty to Tezpore	6
From Tezpore to Bishnath	3
From Bishnath to the mouth of the Dikho river, 12 miles distant from Seebsaugur	6
From Dikhoo Mookh river to Dibroolghur	7
From Dibroolghur to Suddeah or Saikwah	6
Total days	65

Excepting with a westerly wind during the rains, the navigation of the Burrampooter river is tedious, uncertain, and dangerous, from falling banks, floating trees, a rapid current, and no tracking ground: the jungle extending to the edge of the river. In Assam a canoe is the safest and most speedy mode of travelling.

W. Wing del[t].

1. Mangoe Fly.
2. Queen (or Arrindy) Silkworm of Assam.
3. Long Horned Beetle.

Queen silkworm, &c.

CHAPTER II.

Travels and Residence in North-Western Assam.—Description of Burpetah in the Rains.—Vampire, or Fox Bats.—Leaf Insect.—Seclusion of Villages in the Jungles.—Country abounds with Wild Animals.—Number of Deaths, and Damage done to Crops.—Native mode of killing a Tiger.—Conflagrations of Jungles.—Danger therefrom to Travellers.—Cultivation of high and low lands.—Number of Crops.—Primitive Mode of Husbandry.—Irrigation by Cacharies.—Country Inundated.—Population and Condition of the People.—Law on Slavery.

For the more speedy and effective administration of justice among the people residing in the north-west quarter of the district of Kamroop, and for the promotion of trade, the Governor-General's Agent directed the establishment of an outpost for an assistant at Burpetah, on the Chawl Khawa river, and I was selected to proceed for eight months upon this duty.

The population of Burpetah is estimated at about three thousand souls; their huts are built without any regularity on high artificial mounds of earth, in the centre of gardens of betel nut and plantain trees, clumps of bamboos, cane and grass jungle, mango and other large trees, under the shade of which, impervious to the sun, roads or channels intersect the town in every direction. In the rainy season, these channels, owing to the inundation of the country, are filled with water many feet in depth. Every house, consequently, is provided with one or more canoes, in which the inhabitants visit each other's isolated positions; and the cattle are brought upon the little eminences at night, and housed oftentimes under the same roof with the family, if not in the same room. Daily may the cattle be seen swimming across these street-streams in search of a dry spot of land on which to graze. In this manner, for four months of each year—June, July, August, and September—are the people surrounded by floods; but, as if endowed with amphibious natures, they seem equally happy in or out of the water, and pass their time on board their boats in trading with other villages throughout Assam. When at home, they amuse themselves during the rainy season in collecting the wood which floats down the rivers, from the destruction of their banks alluded to in the foregoing chapter; and in the sport of catching wild buffaloes, deer, and pigs, which are now seen in great numbers swimming across the rivers from the low inundated grounds to reach more elevated spots on which to subsist: the animals in their passage, being overtaken by canoes, are captured with the aid of ropes and spears, with little difficulty.

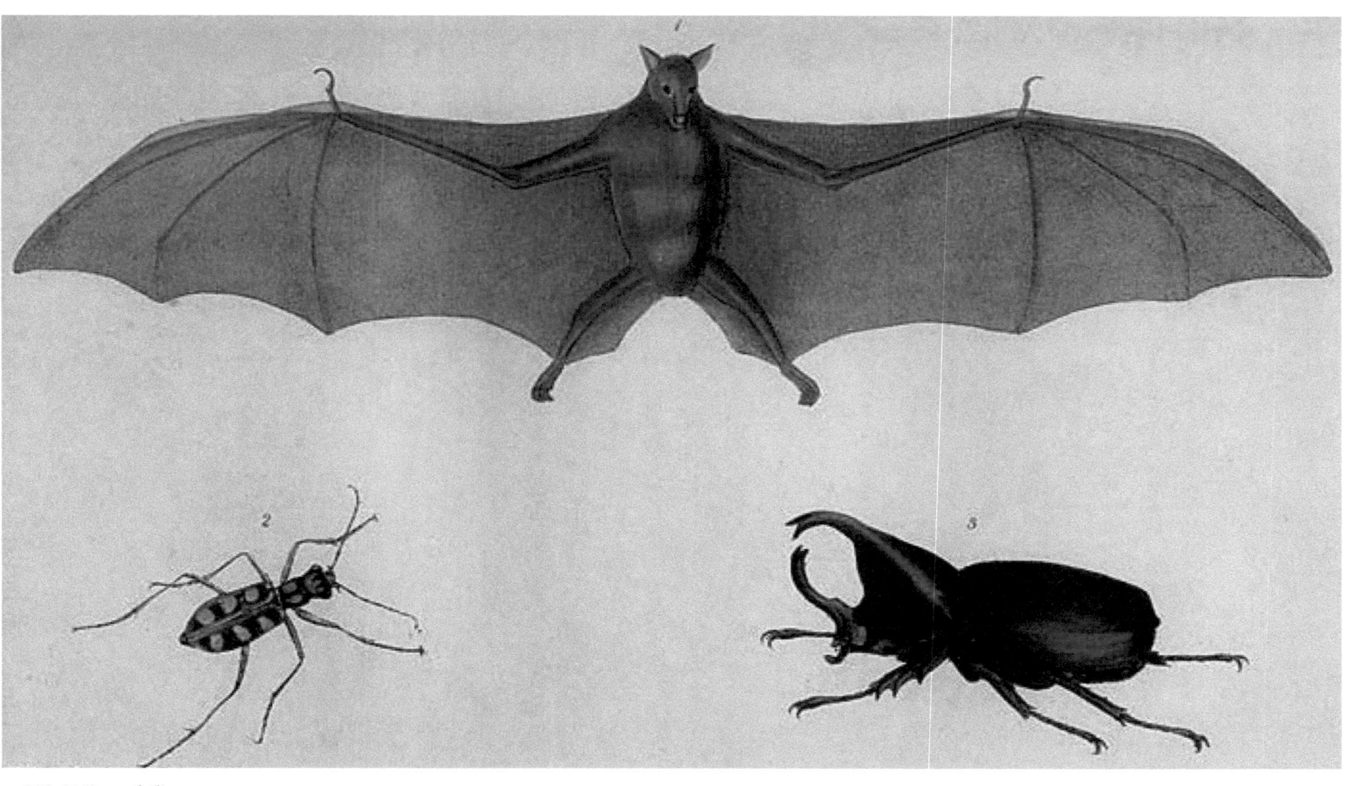

W. Wing del[t].

1. Vampire or Fox Bat.

2. Tiger Beetle of Assam.

3. Hercules Beetle of D[o].

Vampire, or fox bat, &c.

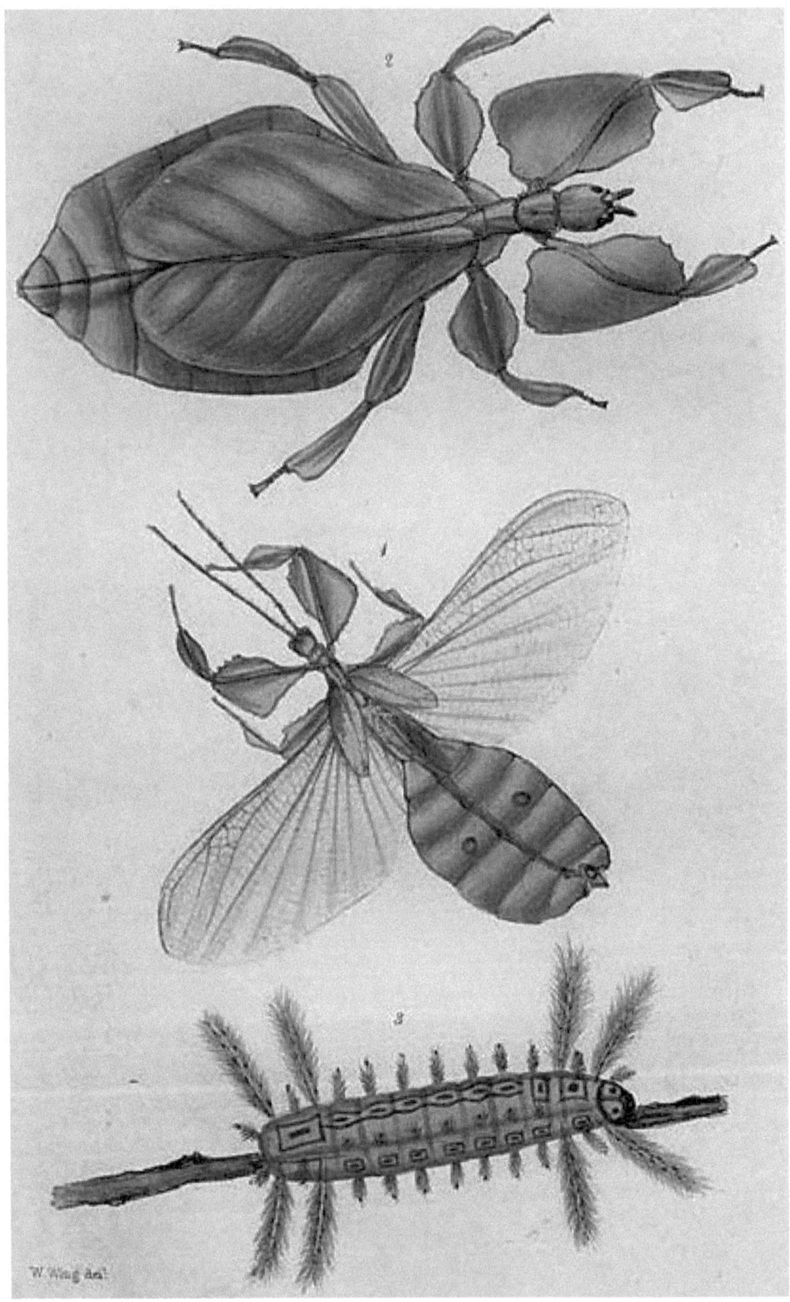

W. Wing del[t].

1 & 2. Leaf Insect of Assam (Male & Female).
3. Saiknah Caterpillar (Butterfly).

Leaf insects

At Burpetah there is a very long building supported by wooden posts carved with emblems of Hindoo Deities, with a grass roof and mat walls. It is called a shuster, alias temple; and is a religious endowment, where the vedas or holy books of the Hindoos are chanted, and offerings in kind and cash received. A grant of rent-free land, given by the Assam king Sebsunker, in 1657 A.S. or 1735 A.D. is attached to the temple, and a number of disciples, with two chief priests or pontiffs, manage the affairs of the establishment.

On the trees at Burpetah, great numbers of the Vampire or Fox-bats are to be seen hanging by their claws with their heads downwards. They are offensive looking objects, having a body eleven inches long, and each wing twenty-two inches in length. I have never heard a native assert that they suck the blood of cattle when sleeping, and if it were the case, such a circumstance would certainly be quickly verified; it may therefore justly be inferred, that this is a popular error. It is said that the food of the fox-bat consists entirely of jungle fruits; their flesh is esteemed a delicacy by many natives, and I have frequently shot them to gratify the appetites of my own servants. There is a strange superstition amongst the natives, that the bones of the fox-bat, worn as an amulet or charm, will cure any limb or part of the body affected with pain.

One of the most curious members of the animal (query, vegetable?) world in Assam is the Leaf insect—so called from its very close resemblance in form, colour, and general structure (even to the fibre), to the leaf of the tree which it inhabits. In fact, until the insect moves, it is difficult to distinguish it from the leaf itself. The annexed drawing will convey an idea of this singular freak of nature; many attempts at transmitting a perfect specimen to Europe have been frustrated by the perishable character of the insect. Spirits are entirely inefficacious as preservatives, and camphor destroys the colour of the animal.

In perambulating the district, I was particularly struck with the immense extent of high grass jungle between the Burrampooter river and the foot of the Bootan mountains. I frequently traversed a distance of eight and ten miles through a dense grass jungle twenty feet high, without meeting with a solitary hut or any cultivation; but suddenly, a village and an open cultivated space of a few hundred acres would burst upon the view and vary the monotony of the scene. This would be followed by a dreary waste extending to the next village, often five or six miles distant; while a solitary foot-path, forming the only communication between the small communities thus isolated, clearly showed that for many months in the year little intercourse, except by water, is kept up between them.

The country is infested with wild animals, and the footpaths are dangerous at all times. Some slight idea may be formed of the danger to human life from the denizens of the jungle, when I state that in the western quarter of the district of Kamroop alone, in the short period of six months, the police reports included twenty men killed by wild elephants and buffaloes. The damage done to the rice crops yearly by wild elephants and buffaloes is very considerable; and although Government bestows a reward of two rupees eight annas, or five shillings, for every buffalo destroyed, and five rupees or ten shillings for every tiger's head, such is the apathy and indifference of the natives to their own interests and preservation, that they seldom exert themselves to earn the gratuity, until repeated aggressions become unbearable. When wild elephants pull down their huts, or a tiger, from previous success, becomes emboldened to enter their little dwellings and carry off their cattle, then the village community will turn out in a body; surrounding with nets the tiger's lair,—a small patch of jungle in the vicinity of the village,—and shouting and yelling, they drive the intruder into the nets, where he falls an easy victim to the spears and bludgeons of the enraged and injured populace.

In January, February, March, and April, the whole country adjoining Burpetah presents a spectacle seldom seen elsewhere: the natives set fire to the jungle to clear the land for cultivation, and to open the thoroughfares between the different villages, and the awful roar and rapidity with which the flames spread cannot be conceived. A space of many miles of grass jungle, twenty feet high, is cleared in a few hours; and the black ashes scattered over the face of the earth after such recent verdure, form one of the most gloomy and desolate landscapes that can well be imagined. But so rapid is vegetation in Assam, that a few days suffice to alter the scene: the jungle speedily shoots up with greater strength than ever, and at the approach of the heavy rains in June, it again attains a height of many feet. On more occasions than one, though mounted on an elephant, I have had the greatest difficulty to out-flank a fierce roaring fire, rapidly moving with the wind, in a long line over the country. The elephant, of all animals, is the most fearful of fire; and on hearing the approach of the element he instantly takes to flight; but the rapidity with which the flames spread renders escape most hazardous, especially if the wind is high and *right aft*. The best plan to adopt if a fire breaks out to windward, is to circle round the nearest flank with all expedition, gaining the space burnt by the advancing flames. On foot, escape would be almost impossible; the jungle being impenetrable except by a narrow footpath, and this being frequently overgrown with grass, if no open spot be near at hand, inevitable destruction must be the fate of any unfortunate traveller to leeward of a fire.

In Assam, excepting the fields close to the villages, the best land is never manured. One crop of planted winter *d'han* or rice is cut in November or December, every year, from generation to generation. This land is never allowed to lie fallow; abundant rain being all that is requisite to ensure plentiful crops: the richness of the soil seems inexhaustible.

The low lands liable to inundation are never manured; the jungle is burnt down, and for three successive years two crops are annually realized from it. In February, mustard seed is gathered in: a source of great profit to the cultivator; and in June the spring rice, sown broad-cast, is reaped. After the land has been thus impoverished, it is allowed to remain fallow for three years; and fresh jungle land is burnt and prepared in the same primitive way, and with the most simple implements of husbandry. In other parts of Assam extensive tracts of land are beautifully cultivated, and pretty villages are numerously studded over the country; but, although lakes and streams are everywhere to be met with, no attempt is made by the Assamese tribes, excepting the Cacharries, to irrigate the land, and thus render the crops more certain and productive.

The Cacharries who reside at the foot of the hills are the most useful and industrious, as well as the most athletic men in Assam, and allowed to be the best cultivators. They irrigate their lands to a great extent from hill streams, and consequently raise far better crops than their neighbours. During the months of June, July, August, and September, a great portion of Assam is inundated, and boats leaving the innumerable streams and large rivers, paddle over the country in every direction; indeed, in many places, particularly at Burpetah, boats form the only means by which any communication can be kept up. To facilitate intercourse during the dry season, roads have been constructed, and bullock-carts introduced, similar to the hackerys in use in the Western Provinces of India, for the conveyance of the produce of the lands to the best markets; but the Assamese are so wedded to their old customs, and attached to the use of slaves and bondsmen in every capacity—as servants, porters, and cultivators, that it has been found no easy matter to induce them to adopt a new system, however obvious its advantages.

A new era, however, is approaching: a law has been promulgated, abolishing slavery in India, and as the people become more enlightened by education and intercourse with Europeans, they will relax their adherence to old and absurd usages and prejudices. In the district of Kamroop above twenty thousand slaves and bondsmen may obtain manumission by simply asking for it; and as there is no doubt they will do so, we may anticipate, from the acquisition of freedom, a total alteration of the habits and feelings of the Assamese. Large wastes of land will be brought under cultivation, and thousands of families made independent and comfortable. Assam has now been subjected to British rule for a period of nearly twenty years, and the people have enjoyed the fruits of their labours in peace and security: a condition of things to which they were strangers under their own chieftains.

The population of Assam is assumed to be about 800,000 souls; but as no correct census has been taken, the accuracy of the estimate cannot be determined. It may be presumed, however, that the population does not increase to any great extent, for a state of slavery and bondage has never been favourable to the due multiplication of the human species.

The proprietors of slaves and bondsmen consist of the most respectable men in Assam, and of course are strenuous supporters of the continuation of the lucrative and nefarious traffic in their fellow-creatures. To deprive them of their proprietary right to their slaves it has been urged would be unjust, and offensive to their usages; and, following the example of the West India proprietors, they contend that the slaves being their lawful property as much as houses, grain, or cattle, compensation should be made by Government for the release of every man from bondage. The Indian Government, however, has adopted a different course. It has published a regulation that forbids the officers of all courts from allowing forcible possession of the person or services of a slave, or his property. In future, therefore, slave-holders will not be able to compel their slaves to obey their orders, and as this law becomes gradually enforced, slavery will be practically abolished; a new order of men will arise, stimulated to more vigorous exertions by the conviction that they will reap the benefit of their labours, and extended cultivation and a freer exchange of commodities will infallibly ensue.

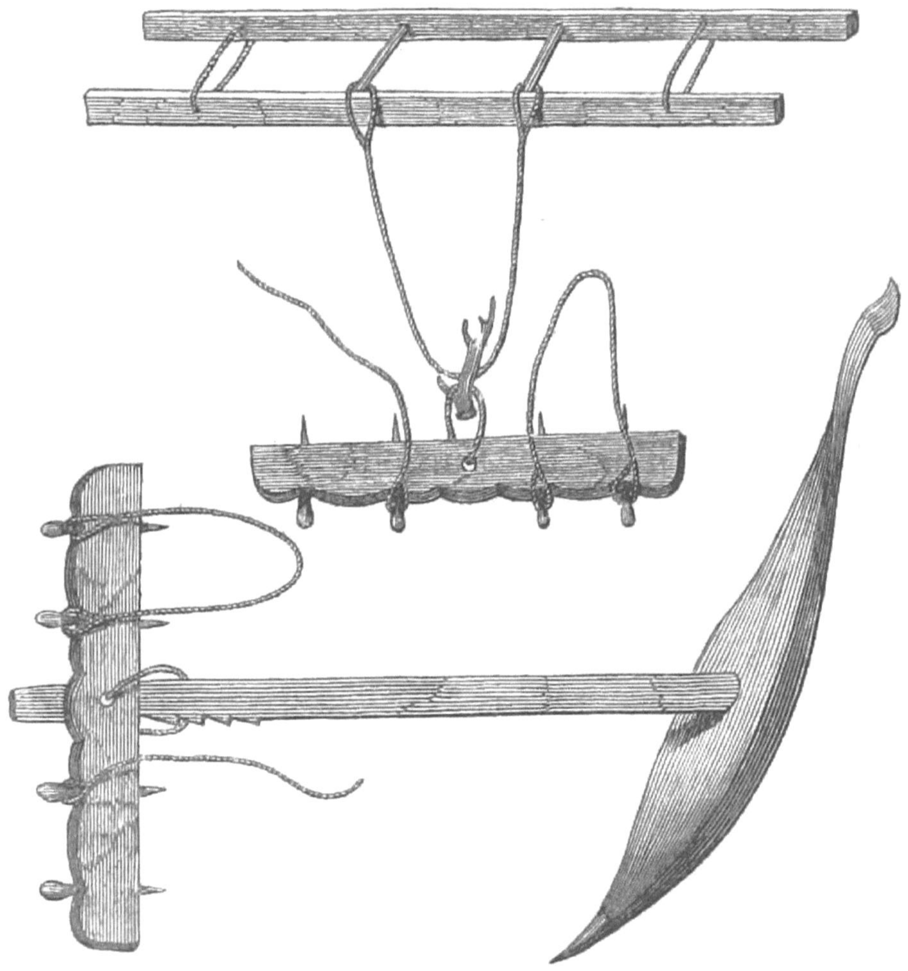

Assamese Plough and Implement for Levelling Ploughed Land.

CHAPTER III.

Forests and Grass Jungle—Tigers, Elephants, Buffaloes, Rhinosceroses, Pigs and Deer—Field Sports by Europeans—Native practice of destroying animals with poisoned arrows—Effects of poison—Wild Elephants caught with a noose in Assam—Secured in a Kheddah or Enclosure at Chittagong—Net Revenue of Assam—Disbursements—Industry—Opium—Slavery—Conclusion.

The enormous extent of forest, and high, dense grass jungle in Assam, exceeds perhaps that of any other country of the same area; and, as a consequence, the herds of wild elephants, buffaloes, deer, rhinosceroses, and tigers, are innumerable. Almost every military officer in civil employ in Assam, having constantly to roam about the country, becomes, if not from choice, at least in self-defence, a keen and skilful sportsman. Herds of one hundred buffaloes each are frequently met with; and though I have known twenty buffaloes shot in one day's diversion, they are so prolific, and the season of four months for sport is so short, that no actual progress appears to be made in the diminution of their numbers. On some occasions, when a buffalo is wounded and unable to escape into high jungle, he furiously charges the elephant on which the sportsman is mounted in a howdah, and often gores the elephant, or injures the feet or legs of the driver seated on the animal's neck, before he can be stopped in his career; for it frequently takes ten or twelve balls to destroy a buffalo, unless an early shot inflicts a vital wound. The elephant, if well trained, on being charged by a buffalo, merely turns round and presents his stern to the repeated blows of the infuriated monster: screaming out, however, in the utmost fright until the buffalo is shot or scared off by the firing; but a timid or badly trained elephant, on being charged instantly seeks safety in flight, to the imminent peril of the sportsman, should any trees happen to come in contact with the howdah. Buffaloes, however, that have been long undisturbed, generally stand still, and with fierce looks and raised horns receive the first few shots in utter astonishment, and then seek shelter in the high jungles with the utmost speed. Rhinosceroses are very numerous in many parts of Assam, and are to be found in very high grass jungle, near inaccessible miry swamps, which preclude pursuit, and having thick skins, they are not easily shot. Elephants dread the charge of a rhinosceros as much as that of a tiger, and the grunting noise of the former animal not unfrequently scares even a well-trained elephant from the field. If the rhinosceros succeeds in overtaking the elephant, he bites large pieces of flesh from the elephant's sides or legs, and with the horn on the nose not unfrequently inflicts fearful wounds. Rhinosceroses are tamed in a few months, and may be seen at Gowahatty grazing on the plains as harmless as cows, attended by a single man. When tamed in Assam they may be bought of the natives for 100 or 150 rupees (10*l.* or 15*l.*); many have been sent to Calcutta, and sold for 500 rupees, or 50*l.*; but the expense of boat hire to the metropolis, provender, and servants' wages, with the risk attendant on the journey to so distant a market, renders the speculation anything but profitable.

Deer shooting is a fine, healthy, exhilarating exercise for those who are not partial to the dangerous and exciting scenes common to tiger, rhinosceros, and buffalo shooting. It is a mistake, however, to suppose it tame, easy sport. Deer shooting requires much practice: a steady foot and arm in a howdah, and a quick sight are indispensable, if you would shoot either pigs or deer while bounding rapidly over the plain.

A most deadly poison is extracted from a kind of root denominated Mishmee Bih (or poison) brought from the Mishmee country, on the north-east quarter of Assam. With this the natives in Upper Assam generally cover the tips of their arrows, and destroy elephants for the sake of the ivory tusks. So powerful, so deadly is the effect of the poison, that the slightest scratch or puncture of an arrow smeared with it proves fatal: if not instantaneously, at all events in a few hours after an elephant has been stricken. Deer and buffaloes are also killed in the same manner. Immediately the animal falls, the wounded part is cut out, and the flesh is then eaten by the natives, without apprehension of any ill effects arising from the inoculation of the body by the poison: at least I have never heard of a single instance of a person losing his life from having eaten of the flesh of animals killed by poisoned arrows, common as is the practice of partaking of such food. Safety appears to be secured by excising the wounded part.

Of all field sports in Assam, that of catching wild elephants with the noose is the most exciting and dangerous. On a herd of wild elephants being discovered, four tame elephants, called *Koonkies*, with two men on each elephant—one sitting on the neck, and called a *Phundaet*, from having to throw the noose, and the other seated on the back, with a club, to urge the elephant into full speed—proceed to join the herd; which generally at first sight of the tame elephants, takes to immediate flight. A good sized wild elephant, however, being quickly selected from the herd by the riders, by common consent, is pursued till fairly run down, when the *Phundaet* throws over the wild elephant's head a large rope noose, one end of which is attached to the body of the tame elephant on which he is mounted, and the wild animal is instantly pulled up and rendered helpless. The other three tame elephants now joining, another noose is thrown over the wild elephant's head on the other side; the ropes on both sides being extended to a distance of ten paces. The entangled brute is then triumphantly led off between the two tame elephants to a place of security, where, his legs being bound with ropes to a large post in front and rear, he is kept on low diet until he becomes tractable,—a state to which he submits himself in an incredibly short space of time. The female elephants may, in two months, be driven alone anywhere; but the male elephants take four, six, and sometimes twelve months before they can be trusted to walk alone, unhampered with ropes. When a male elephant, with tusks, becomes entangled with the noose round his neck—which noose, by the way, has a knot to prevent strangulation—the animal frequently rushes down with the utmost ferocity on the tame elephants, and with his tusks gores them in a most frightful manner. In such a case it becomes necessary to quickly bind his legs with large ropes, and no further resistance is then of any avail. The individuals who throw the noose over the wild elephant's head are oftentimes in the most imminent danger, but their agility in shifting their position to any part of the body of the tame elephant, enables them to elude injury. The tractability and sagacity of the tame elephant in making every effort to secure the wild elephant by putting the ropes round his legs, is very remarkable. Indeed, so cunning are the tame elephants,—so intuitive is their apprehension of their duty—that there is little difficulty in capturing the wild elephant.

It is calculated that not less than five hundred elephants are yearly caught in Assam and sent to Western India for sale. At Chittagong, in the south-eastern quarter of Bengal, the mode of catching wild elephants is very different from that adopted in Assam. Herds of fifty elephants are there surrounded by two or three hundred men, the jungle is filled, and a regular barricade of trees, with a trench, formed; the elephants are thus unable to break loose; tame elephants are then sent into the enclosure, which is called a Keddah, and the wild elephants are quickly secured with ropes.

The formation of these enclosures is a work of great labour and considerable expense; but the Government are amply repaid by the sale of about one hundred elephants annually, caught in this manner. Chittagong elephants are considered very superior to those caught in Assam, the former being stout, strong, short-legged beasts, and the latter lanky and weak; but whether the prejudice be just, may be doubted, as there are many noble elephants in Assam that would prove most serviceable in any part of India, and the prices they would fetch amply repay any charge incurred by Government for an elephant-hunting establishment in Assam.

The annual sum expended for the support of civil and military establishments in Assam cannot, I suspect (for I have no documents to refer to), be less than 700,000 rupees, 70,000*l*. And the net revenue derived from six districts exhibited in the following table[1] is rupees 611,268 9 7, showing that the disbursements exceed the receipts. This is to be regretted, for disinterested individuals conclude that Assam might be made a source of profit instead of expense to the Government, without the smallest possible risk of the peace of the north-eastern frontier of India not being maintained in security. But were it otherwise, the sum yearly expended in excess of the net revenue for the management of Assam, it must be borne in mind, is not thrown away, for Assam forms the best frontier protection for Bengal that could be desired; and if troops were not located in that province, a force would be required on the north eastern frontier, involving much heavier expense than the Local Corps of Assam. Every endeavour, therefore, to promote the advancement and civilization of the people of Assam must be hailed as a favourable omen of future prosperity.

---

[1] Page 24.

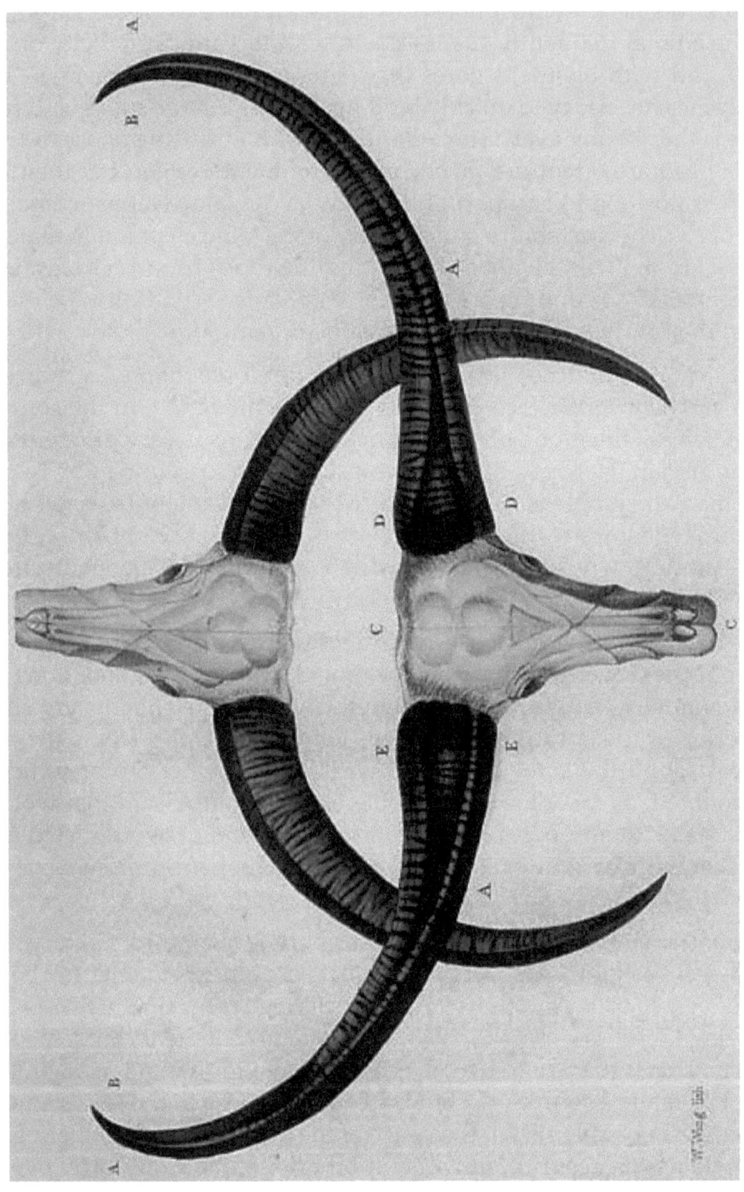

W. Wing lith.

AAAA. Round the outside of the Horns & across the forehead 12 F.[t] 2 Inches. B to B In direct line 6 F.[t] 8½ Inches. C to C. 2 Feet 4 Inches.

D to D Circumference of Right Horn. 1 Foot 8½ Inches. E to E. Circumference of Left Horn: 1 Foot 8 Inches. Across the Forehead 11 Inches.

The Horns do not correspond in length & shape.

Buffalo heads in Assam.

Buffalo shooting in Assam.

The utter want of an industrious, enterprising spirit, and the general degeneracy of the Assamese people, are greatly promoted by the prevalent use of opium; they would rather consent to be deprived of food than their accustomed dose of this deleterious drug, and so emaciated and weakened have many become from indulging in its use, that they are unequal to any great exertion, either mental or bodily, until the usual stimulating dose has been imbibed. Government have established no regulations against the growth of opium in Assam, neither do they derive any greater revenue from its cultivation than is yielded them by other lands. It cannot be doubted that, if a heavy tax were levied on every acre of land producing opium, and a high duty imposed on its sale, it would be beyond the means of the people to purchase and consume such quantities of the drug, as is now the practice of men, women, and even children. The consequence would be that in a few years many would be weaned from their predilection for the pernicious opiate, which at present is esteemed a sovereign remedy for every evil in life. Notwithstanding the degraded state of the Assamese population, we may yet regard Assam as a rising country; the price of all commodities, as well as the wages of labour, having been greatly enhanced under the British rule.

In concluding these brief notes on Assam, justice, gratitude, and esteem, require that the personage holding the exalted dignity of the Governor-General's agent in Assam, Major Francis Jenkins, should be presented to the notice of the reader. It is to him the English public are largely indebted for forming the grand scheme of supplying his native country with tea from Assam. It is to his able and persevering exertions, during a ten years' sojourn, that the affairs of Assam, both in a political and financial view, have been retrieved from almost inextricable disorder. Before Major Jenkins arrived, very few officers were allowed to conduct the political duties of the province; and these gentlemen being, moreover, overwhelmed with other business, improvements could not be contemplated: the current routine of fiscal and criminal duties was all that two or three individuals could be expected to superintend. This state of affairs was remedied by Major Jenkins, who pointed out to Government the indisputable advantages that would accrue from a more liberal policy being pursued in aiding him with a greater number of European assistants. His representations were acceded to; the revenue has consequently increased, and the people, as far as their vices will permit, have thriven in peace, security, and comfort. The British Government has relieved Assam from the barbarous mutilations, cruel impalements, and other outrages against humanity which its inhabitants were subject to under their ancient rulers; and distress, anarchy, or discontent amongst our own subjects in Assam is unknown. A few petty aggressions of savage hill tribes occasionally occur, demanding constant vigilance and prompt suppression, but with this exception, peace and plenty prevail throughout the valley; and when the day arrives for Major Jenkins's departure from Assam to his native land, that liberal, benevolent, and highly-gifted man will be much regretted by his European assistants, and by the native population of the province, all of whom look up to him as a protector and friend.

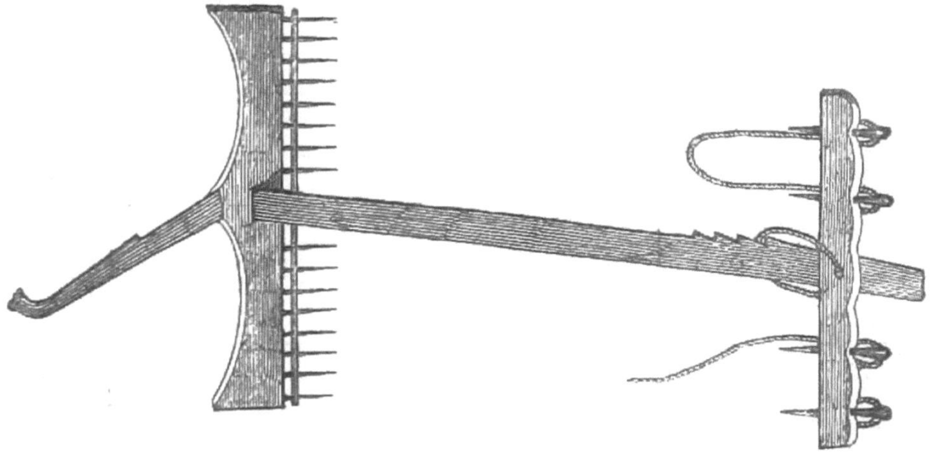

Assamese harrow for thinning and cleaning Paddy.

STATISTICS OF ASSAM.

No. of Districts.	Names of Districts in Assam.	Governor General's Agent North East Frontier. Military Officer.	Deputy Commr. of Assam. Military Officer.	Principal Assistants to the Governor General's Agent. Military Officers.	Junior Assistants to the Governor General's Agent. Military Officers.	Sub-Assistants to the Governor General's Agent. Uncovenanted Officers.	Native Sudder Ameens or Judges to try cases not exceeding 1000 rupees.	Native Moonsiffs or Judges to try cases under 300 rs.	Net Revenue of each District in Assam. Co's. Rupees.	Ans.	Pice.
1	Kamroop	...	...	1	1	1	1	6	252991	3	6
2	Durrung	...	...	1	1	1	1	3	142299	1	0
3	Nowgong	...	...	1	...	2	1	1	103925	2	5
4	Seebsaugur	...	...	1	...	2	1	2	70135	10	5
5	{ Luckimpoor	...	...	1	1	1	1	1	14131	12	0
	{ Muttuck	...	...	...	...	...	...	...	16950	0	0
6	Goalparah	...	...	1	...	1	1	1	10835	12	3
6		1	1	6	3	8	6	14	611268	9	7

SOME ACCOUNT
OF
THE ASSAMESE TRIBES.

Observations on the Khamtees—Surprise and Conflagration of the Station of Suddeah by the Khamtees, in January 1839—Singphoos—Muttucks—State of Assam Tea Company—Bor Abors—Abors and Merees—Mishmees—Dooaneahs—Assamese—Nagas—American Baptist Missionaries in Assam—Garrows—Their present and eventual condition—Cosseahs—Traits of the people of Bootan—Attachment of the Bootan Dooars in Assam by the British Government—Defeat of the Booteahs, in 1836—Sath Booteah Rajahs of Kooreahparah Dooar, in Durrung—Thebingeah Booteah Rajahs—Sath Rajahs of Char Dooar—Hazaree Khawa Akhas—Kuppah Choor Akhas—Meechees, and Dufflahs of Now Dooar.

KHAMTEES.

THE KHAMTEES: their subjection of Suddeah and Saikwah—Their defeat and expulsion—Re-establishment of their authority at Suddeah and Saikwah—Intrigues and disaffection to the British Government in 1820—Captain Charlton placed in charge of the Khamtee chiefs at Suddeah and Saikwah, 1834–35—Attempts of the Khamtees in 1837–38 to subvert British authority—Their insurrection in 1839, and attack on the post at Suddeah and repulse—Death of Lieutenant White—Expulsion of the Khamtees from Assam—Their submission and pardon—Character and habits of the Khamtees

In the reign of Rajeswur Sing, Rajah of Assam, about 1751 A.D., on the north-eastern frontier of Assam, the Khamtees, it is traditionally reported, emigrated from a range of mountains bordering on the sources of the Irawaddy river to the valley of Assam, and settled a small colony of fifteen houses in the vicinity of the Tengapanee river. But between the years 1780 and 1794 A.D., Goureenath Sing, the reigning Rajah of Assam, was compelled to abandon Upper Assam after repeated battles with the rebellious Moamareahs of Muttuck, and in the anarchy that prevailed throughout the country, the Khamtees were emboldened to take up a more advanced position. For that purpose, being joined by another band of 400 Khamtees with some few muskets, they fearlessly located themselves at Suddeah; and, though nominally subordinate to the Assam Government, they arrogantly exercised considerable power over the people of the Suddeah and Saikwah districts: which were exceedingly populous at that period, and had been placed under the direct authority of an Assamese nobleman, styled Suddeah Khawa, an Ahoom by birth. Not content with this usurpation, they proceeded to reduce the whole of the Assamese population to the utmost verge of degradation; considering them as slaves, only worthy to be spared so long as they continued obedient to the will, and were useful to their masters in cultivating the land, and contributing to their comforts. In the height of their success, promoted by the weakness of the Assam Government, the Khamtees commenced kidnapping the Merees, and other inhabitants settled in the neighbourhood of the Dehong and Debong rivers, whom the Abors looked on as their dependants and slaves, entitled to their special protection. This treatment being less endurable than that of the Abors, towards whom a friendly feeling had been created by long intercourse, the Merees were induced to implore the protection of the latter to save them from being cruelly taken away from their homes to serve as slaves amongst a strange tribe. The Abors, on their side, perceiving that they were about to lose the greater portion of their slaves by the aggressions of a formidable foe, lost no time in preparing for war; and descending from their mountain fastnesses to the plains bordering on the Dehong river, a furious battle was fought between them, and, it is said, two or three hundred Khamtees. The contest terminated in the Khamtees being defeated and dispersed with great slaughter, upwards of one hundred men being left on the field of battle. This trial of strength and courage with their warlike neighbours, rendered the Khamtees ever afterwards more circumspect in their demeanour towards the Abors, and the people subject to them.

During the reign of Kumleswur Sing Rajah, from 1794 to 1809, frequent battles were fought between the royal troops and Khamtees, and generally to the discomfiture of the latter. In fact so disastrous to the Khamtees were the results, that the whole tribe was dispersed; many were detained prisoners, and the remainder were compelled to quit Suddeah and return to the country whence they had issued. In 1810, Chunderkant Rajah ascended the throne, and in the commencement of his reign the Khamtees endeavoured to regain their lost position. Joining the Singphoos at Suddeah, they attacked one of the forts situated at the foot of the northern hills above Suddeah, commanded by Bihitea Burrah and Kooch Burrah, and were successful in a night assault, having destroyed the fortress by fire and massacred 150 soldiers. They were, however, speedily repulsed by the Assam troops, and the whole clan was thenceforth expelled the province.

In 1816–17, Chunderkant Rajah was treacherously invited by the Borax Gohain to visit Jorehath, where he was formally deposed, and ignominiously treated: having one of his ears slit, which disqualified him for regal dignities; and Poorunder Sing, the great grandson of Rajeswur Sing Rajah, was duly installed in his seat. This arrangement, however, was of short duration, for in 1818 a Burmese army of 30,000 men invaded Assam and replaced Chunderkant on his throne. The ex-Rajah, Poorunder Sing, on this sudden and unlooked for change of affairs, prudently retired to Chilmary, in Bengal.

Under the Burmese Government, the Assamese at Suddeah were placed under a Khamtee Gohain, or chief; and when the province was conquered in 1824–25, Captain Neufville sanctioned the innovation, bestowing on a Khamtee chief the title of Suddeah Khawa. But the rights of the Assam *régime* had devolved on the British Government, with whom it rested to revert to the former rule wherever it might be deemed expedient: and that without any injustice to the Khamtees, as they had no claim whatever to the title in question. The assumption of the title of Suddeah Khawah, by the Khamtees is variously described. It is currently believed that Chunderkant Rajah—feeling himself insecure on the throne whilst he had to contend with the Boora Gohain and the ex-Rajah Poorunder Sing—invited the Khamtees to return to Suddeah, and bestowed on one of the Khamtee chiefs the title of Suddeah Khawa; in order, by this arrangement, to secure, through their means, a retreat for himself, if unfortunate at a future day. But in 1820 A.D., the Burphokun having been murdered, with the connivance, it was supposed, of Rajah Chunderkant, the Burmese became his enemies, and returned and dethroned him, shortly afterwards, placing on the throne Jugesur Sing, who was the last prince of the Assam dynasty. In this interval of anarchy, the Khamtees had re-established their influence and power to such an extent as to overawe almost the whole of the tribes of the frontier; and their authority at Suddeah was paramount. The Assamese, though greatly reduced in numbers by oppression and deaths, and from being carried off and sold into slavery by the Singphoos and Burmese, were all now permanently under the control of the Khamtees; but on the submission of the latter to the British Government, a settlement was made with them, leaving the internal management of the tribes to their own chiefs, who were exempt from taxation, but under the obligation of performing military service to the state when required. Revenue, however, was to be paid for the Assamese subjects under their management, and cases of murder, wounding, arson, and petty thefts above fifty rupees were disposed of by British officers.

The military population of the Suddeah district, on the north bank of the Burrampooter, was estimated at this period to be—Assamese, 691, Khamtees, 428, men capable of bearing arms: multiply these numbers by three, for old men, women, and children, we shall reach a census of 4476 souls. On the south bank, in the district of Saikwah, according to the same calculation, there were,—Assamese, 616, Khamtees, 248, which, with old men, women, and children, amounted in all to 3456 persons; thus making the united population on the north and south banks of the Burrampooter, in the districts of Suddeah and Saikwah, 7,932 persons.

In the year 1829, notwithstanding the Khamtees were bound by treaty to pay allegiance to the British Government, such was the intriguing character of the Khamtee Suddeah Khawa Gohain, that the strongest ground existed for believing him to be engaged in a traitorous combination against us. He was the first person who invited the Burmese into the country, and having a relative residing at Ava, he maintained not only with that court, but throughout the frontier, a general correspondence. In the absence of a European military officer, or Political Agent at Suddeah, a native manager or Suznatee, was generally the channel of all communications between the chiefs and the British Government. But in the years 1834–35, Captain Charlton was placed in charge of the Khamtee chiefs, and the Suddeah and Saikwah districts; and by the measures he adopted to check the traffic in slaves, and protect the Assam population from the oppressive exactions of the Khamtees, he created the utmost dissatisfaction among the latter, and caused them to be highly incensed. Moreover, in December 1834, instructions were issued requiring a census of the population to be taken; with the view of levying a capitation tax, to be renewed every five years, in lieu of military service to the state. When this innovation was proposed, it was urged that the state of society among these tribes was such, that the materials for direct taxation were not available; that the introduction of our rule would cause too violent a shock to the habits and usages of the rude people; and that the result, in all probability, would be a harassing rebellion, which would retard the progress of improvement. Concurring in these views, the Government deemed it unsafe fully to enforce the plan of assessment. The Assamese residing within the Suddeah territory were taxed at the rate of one rupee per head; but the Khamtee tribes were exempted from this imposition, on condition of their performing military service as they had hitherto done under the

Assamese and British Governments.

Notwithstanding this concession, however, an insubordinate spirit was immediately manifested by the tribes, and it thus became necessary to deprive them of the muskets given them by Captain Neufville, and to depose the Khamtee Suddeah Khawa Gohain. The loss of this title and usurped sovereignty over the Assamese was grievously felt by the Khamtees, and from that period their estrangement from the British Government may fairly be dated. About this time, also, the Khamtee Suddeah Khawa Gohain was arraigned on a charge of slave-dealing,—an unfortunate occurrence, which rendered the Khamtee chiefs still more indisposed to our rule. Serious apprehensions were thenceforth entertained of an open revolt, and combination with our enemies. Nevertheless, not to appear distrustful of their intentions, they were invited to accompany Lieut. Charlton, in the rainy season of 1835, in the expedition against the Duffa Gaum's force at the stockade of Gackwah; in storming which place the Runowa, the Tow Gohain of Derack (who was wounded in the neck), and the Captain Gohain accompanied him, and were said to have behaved bravely, and been present when Lieut. Charlton was wounded. It was confidently asserted, however, that though these chiefs did accompany Lieut. Charlton when he took the advanced stockade or guard-house, there were not more than five or six men in it, who ran away immediately; and it is probable that the Khamtee chiefs were aware of there being so few men, as they afterwards completely abandoned Lieut. Charlton when he so gallantly attacked the large stockade. Indeed, from the whole of their conduct subsequently, there is every reason to conclude that they were in league with the enemy, for they made no attempt to obstruct his retreat, and said openly that they could not be expected to fight now that a census was taking of their subjects for the purpose of assessing them; and that they got no presents as was formerly the custom. In the cold season of 1835, the Political Agent led another expedition against the Duffa Gaum, and accepted the voluntary offer of the Khamtee chiefs to accompany him: not in a well-grounded belief in the sincerity of the proposal, but as a matter of policy, with the view of rendering the Duffa Gaum doubtful of their intentions; and thinking it safer to keep an eye upon them, whilst close at hand, rather than to leave them in the rear. In these operations, all previous suspicions of their disaffection were completely confirmed, for in no one instance did the principal chiefs afford any support, and they even took care not to place their contingents within fire on the first day. Subsequently, when placed on the line of the Duffa Gaum's retreat, they made no effort to obstruct it, otherwise the chief would have been captured; and there is every reason to believe that the negoctiation was entirely defeated through their efforts, in concert with others.

The difficulty, however, of substantiating matters of this kind in this frontier, amongst these wild tribes, is exceedingly great, for a great deal of correspondence on such subjects is carried on by symbols and tokens: such as pieces of buffalo flesh, short swords, muskets, ball, powder, &c.; but at the very time the Khamtees were posted to cut off the Duffa Gaum's retreat, one of their chiefs deserted to him, and doubtless gave the intelligence the enemy stood in need of; and it is currently reported that they fired on the British troops, with whom they were co-operating, more than on the enemy. It is even believed that the Khamtees were aware of the Duffa Gaum's irruption from the first, and promoted it, with the view of finding us occupation on the frontier, and thereby preventing the realization of our plans for assessing them, as they were firmly impressed with the belief that it was our intention to reduce them to a level with the Assamese. It is true that they offered to pay taxes at one rupee per head, on condition of being exempted from military service, but that they were sincere in this offer was not credited: had the measure been enforced, they would probably have resisted it, or moved out of our territory.

In the beginning of 1837, a marked spirit of disaffection existed amongst the Khamtee chiefs, and it was generally understood that they had combined with the Abors and Mishmees to subvert our power; and they had probably encouraged the Abors to attack us, in the hope of making themselves of consequence and thereby recovering their former power over the Assamese. Or it might have been with a view of preventing the extension of taxation to themselves, which, notwithstanding our promises to the contrary, they expected would be enforced when necessary or convenient. In the latter end of 1837, the Khamtees made an inroad on the Mishmees, averring that the Mishmees had taken away their slaves some years ago; but there is no record of the existence of any real pretext for violence. On the contrary, it appears that the Khamtees sold the subjects of the British Government to the Mishmees. The real motive for the incursion is supposed to have been that the Runoah and Tawah Gohains intended proceeding to a particular spot in the Mishmee hills, with the view of expelling a portion of that tribe and of ultimately withdrawing themselves from the authority of the British Government, to which they had evinced no cordial feeling of attachment. In fact, both in 1835 and 1837 it was recommended to the Government that the Khamtees should be located elsewhere than at Suddeah, in order that unpleasant collisions might be avoided, and our peaceable Assamese subjects be induced more cheerfully to submit to taxation.

The only incident that transpired worthy of notice in 1838 was that, without any permission, the Khamtees commenced preparing some lands for cultivation about a day's journey from Suddeah; alleging as their reason the scarcity of good land at Suddeah. This plea was, however, untenable: the real cause was that the paucity of the population at Suddeah had rendered it necessary for the Government officers to make requisitions for coolies to work on the roads, although considerably higher wages had been paid than in other parts of the country, and the dread of these requisitions had induced the Khamtees to think of removing.

Thus passed the years 1836, 37 and 38: rumours of an insurrection being about to break out were occasionally prevalent, but it was supposed that the Khamtees had too much good sense to league with other lawless and disaffected tribes and hazard a rebellion, unless supported by a large Burmese army. In the following year, however, the deceitful calm was suddenly disturbed. About half past 2 o'clock on the morning of the 28th January, 1839, the clouds that had long been gathering, burst on the doomed post of Suddeah. The Khamtees, including a few Moolooks and Singphoos and others, in number about six hundred fighting men, divided into four parties—impressed with their own importance and strength, and perhaps stimulated to greater daring by opium—insidiously set fire to the houses of the officers and huts of the soldiers and camp followers, at different points; at the same time furiously attacking with short swords, spears, &c., the stockade and Assam Light Infantry in their lines, and the quarters of the artillery. Notwithstanding that the attack was totally unlooked for, and the greatest confusion prevailed from the extensive conflagration and uproar throughout the station—the Sipahees being surrounded by their wives and families, and knowing that the enemy cut up men, women, and children, indiscriminately—the panic was of short duration. Discipline soon came into play; a few men got together, headed by their officers, and retook the stockade in fifteen minutes. The enemy then confined their remaining exertions to cutting up a few helpless individuals in the bazaar; but after a few rounds of grape and round shot from a carronade and a six-pounder which had been fired, at the commencement of the attack, they fled from the cantonment of Suddeah in three bodies, leaving behind them twenty-one men killed on the spot. The loss of killed and wounded on our side, including men, women, and children, amounted to eighty persons. The political agent, Lieutenant-Colonel White, who had only arrived at Suddeah a few days before the attack, placing too much confidence in the illusive permanence of Khamtee allegiance, did not deem it necessary to have for his protection a guard of Sipahees at his house; and on this eventful night he had left his bungalow on the first alarm, and was proceeding by the nearest route to the lines, when he was met by a party of the enemy, who instantly attacked him. He fell, pierced with nine spear wounds. It is a matter of great regret that this officer should have lost his life from the want of proper precaution, for, had a guard been placed at his house, there is little doubt but that he would have fought his way in safety to the troops in the lines, as other officers did. Being a benevolent, brave, talented officer, his death was deeply lamented by the corps; more particularly as he was the only European who met an untimely end on this memorable morning.

The Khamtees, it is reported, had long endeavoured to persuade the Singphoos to join them in their intended outbreak and massacre of our troops, and some had assented to share in the promised plunder of the district; but whether they hesitated from fear of the consequences, or that the Khamtees anticipated the day of attack from a sanguine expectation of accomplishing their design through their own prowess, unassisted by other tribes, we had no means of ascertaining: further than that the Singphoos, excepting a few in the neighbourhood of Suddeah, on this occasion showed their foresight and prudence in not being implicated in the reckless rebellion. But as the Singphoos, immediately after the Suddeah catastrophe, attacked and burnt several villages in the Saikwah district, it is evident they were prepared to take advantage of the surprise of the post had our troops been defeated or annihilated.

The Moolooks engaged in this conspiracy were well affected to the British Government, and at first refused to join the Khamtees in attacking our troops; but the Moolook Gaum, or chief, having been instantly barbarously murdered by the Khamtees for declining to act against us, his little band was intimidated and compelled reluctantly to follow the dreaded Khamtee leaders. A few Mishmees, who were also at this time on a visit to Suddeah for trading purposes, were unfortunately induced to join in the treacherous affray, and many that were fighting for their lives were slain by the troops. Some of the Suddeah Assamese population were likewise implicated, and punished by the law with the severity their temerity and ingratitude deserved: for they had received no provocation, neither had they any grievances to resent or redress.

In a few months the Khamtee tribe (excepting the Khamtees of Palangpan, who were not implicated) were driven by the Assam Light Infantry beyond the frontier; and the Assam valley was, for the third time within a century, freed from the presence of this inimical tribe. Shortly after the return of the troops from this expedition, however, the Khamtees again located themselves at the foot of the Mishmee hills, close to a pass leading into the Burkhamtee country. In 1843, the Runoah Gohain and Tow Gohain, chief actors in the dire disaster of 1839, being dead, their sons and many Khamtees, sent in a petition for pardon, and for permission to return and place themselves under the protection of the British Government. Their prayer was generously acceded to, and a treaty was at once drawn up offering them free pardon for the past rebellion: on condition of their coming down with their wives and families and locating themselves at Choonpoorah, a short distance above Suddeah, where they should be permitted to cultivate the land rent free for five years. They were further bound to abstain from the trafficking in slaves, and to arrange all petty disputes amongst themselves; but all heinous offences, murder, gang robbery, serious wounding and thefts, were to be settled by the political agent. Finally, after ten years they were to abide by any other arrangement the British Government might deem expedient. Previous to this settlement, and shortly after the insurrection of 1839, a small body of Khamtees were sent down to the district of Luckimpore, and by their own industry cleared and brought into a beautiful state of cultivation a fine tract of country. They, however, live most secludedly from their neighbours, retaining their own habits and customs; and it is to be feared that a long period of time will elapse before they amalgamate or assimilate themselves with the Assamese population. Eventually, should the whole body of this discontented, restless, intriguing tribe return to their allegiance under the British Government, their past history would not warrant the most sanguine mind to expect from them, permanently, either a cheerful submission to our rule or a readiness to pay revenue, without an exhibition of force. Neither can we confidently anticipate that they will adopt peaceable, agricultural, industrious habits in the present generation; being addicted to opium and habitual indolence, and preferring the precarious gain derivable from bartering ivory, gold, and impure silver, to the drudgery of regular industry. But it is impossible to calculate on the benefits and changes that might be effected in their feelings and character, could they be prevailed on to have their children educated in our schools; and this scheme for their amelioration has long been contemplated.

In stature the Khamtees are middle sized, in countenance resembling the Chinese more than any other tribe on the frontier, and possessing the same kind of complexion: perhaps a shade darker. They are an active, intelligent, shrewd, warlike looking race of men, but there is a sinister expression, mixed with a peculiar severity, pervading their countenances, that leaves anything but a favourable impression of the benevolence of their dispositions. Vindictive and cruel natures would infallibly be imputed to them by the physiognomist, and experience has shown that this would prove a just estimate of their general character. The chiefs of this tribe are fond of mechanical employments, and with rude instruments most ingeniously work up iron and silver into a variety of forms for arms, ornaments, and pipes. With a little European instruction they would probably become skilful workmen in this art. Their wearing apparel consists of a simple dhotee or sheet folded round the waist and falling below the knee; this, with a dyed blue cotton jacket extending below the waist and well fitted to the body, gives them a smart, tidy appearance. Their long hair is bound up in a high knot on the crown of the head, and sometimes a white cotton cloth is used as a turban. The principal food of the Khamtees consists of rice and vegetables; but meat, when procurable, is never refused. They also enjoy spirituous liquors; and their creed, Boodhism, seems to have imbued them with few prejudices debarring them from the unrestrained indulgence of their natural inclinations.

SINGPHOOS.

THE SINGPHOOS: their country, population, chiefs and clans—Their dislike of British powers—Their subjection in 1826—Terms of treaty—Feud between two rival chieftains—Submission and subsequent flight of the Duffa Gaum—Disaffection of Tengapanee Singphoos—Tour of the political agent—Fresh disturbances—Character of the country and people—Their religion, customs, and condition—Capabilities for commerce—Government experiment in the woollen trade—Boundary of Assamese and Burmese territories

"'Tis ours by craft and by surprise to gain:—
'Tis theirs to meet in arms and battle on the plain." PRIOR.

The Singphoo tribes occupy the country between the twenty-eighth and twenty-ninth degrees of north latitude, bounded on the north by the Burrampooter, on the east by the Mishmee mountains, on the south by the Patkoe range, and on the west by the space from the mouth of the Now Dehing river, debouching into the Burrampooter in a direct line to Ningroo, terminating at the foot of the hills south of the Boree Dehing river. Half of this tract, of about 1,400 square miles, may be considered hilly, and the remainder undulating. The soil is rich and fertile, and abundant crops of rice are easily raised both on the high and low lands. Sugar-cane grows luxuriantly; tea is likewise found, and every part of the country is intersected by fine clear streams. The most productive corn tracts are the valleys of the Teerap, Namroop, Boree Dehing, Now Dehing, Mudhoopanee, Tengapanee, and Kurempanee. Almost the whole of this country, at the present time, may be said to be one immense forest, but about sixty years ago, or previous to the arrival and settlement of the Singphoos within the Assam frontier, it was considered, from the great extent of cultivation, a fertile, salubrious region. The Singphoo population was estimated in 1838 at about 6000 persons; but in the absence of a regular census, we can form no accurate estimate of their real numbers. At the present day their communities are very small: probably 6000 persons would not be found scattered over the whole frontier north of the Patkoe range. In the vicinity of the Tengapanee, the following Singphoo chiefs reside:—Niphoonnong, Tangsangtau, Jowbongsang, Nidong, Koonkie, Phoop, Oompheedor, Luttora, Ong, Keemingdoo, Niyang, Lajee, Mannong, Nakinchong, Nisah, Koomiyunglah, Ninayong, Jooloo, Nisah Doboon, Jowna, Wakhut. On the Now Dehing; Komonjong, Wakhut, Soanjang, Kamchowjow. On the Mudhoo and Jengloo-Panee; Luthaon-Jowbong, Simaen, Moolan, Jowken, Nisam, Phoinchee, Seerolasein, Mokhoh, Nidhen Lekhala, Nizen Chowkhen. On the Boree Dhing; Kinglong, Chamsong, Ningroola, Beesa, Lakhoom, Noobrong, Lajong, Seong, Bathamgam, Moongong, Jowkeem.

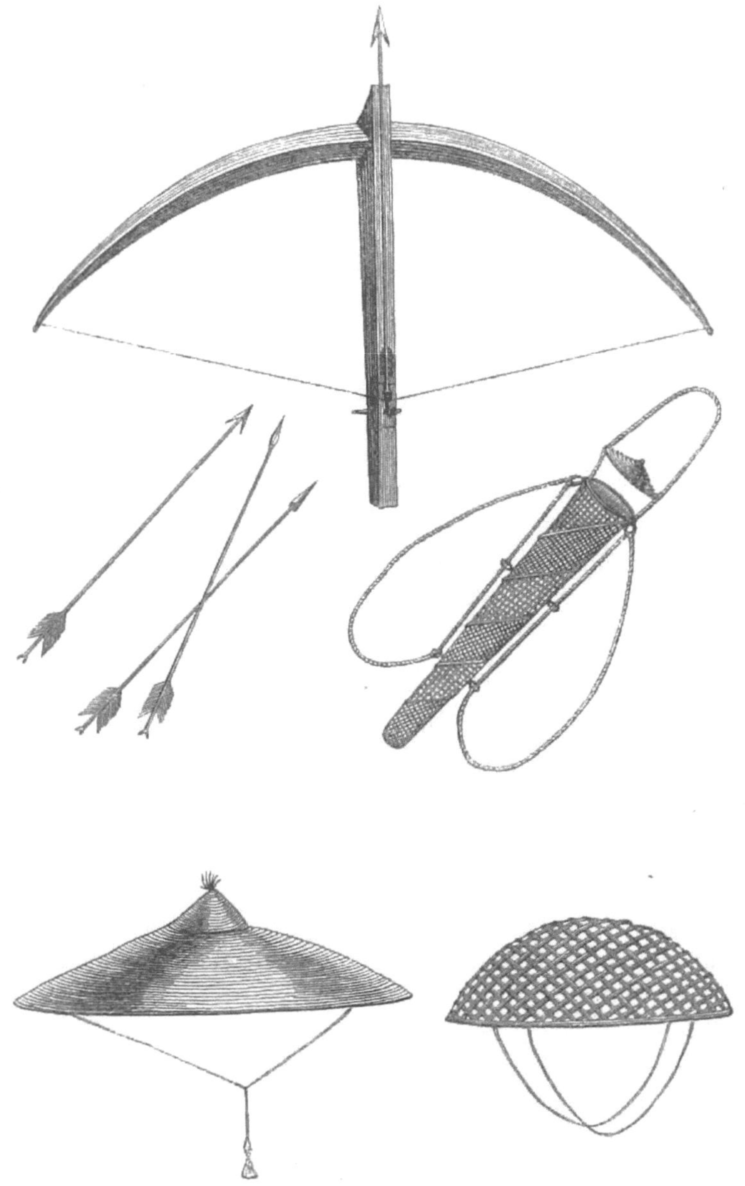

Singphoo Hat, helmet, Cross-bow, Quiver, and arrows.

Each of the different Singphoo tribes is governed by a chief, designated a Gaum, whose authority over his clan is nearly despotic, and entirely independent of the other chiefs. The general body of clans seldom combine, except for purposes of plunder. Occasionally, however, some chiefs, endowed with superior energy, acquire influence over the rest; and this would appear to have been the case with the Beesa Gaum, when the late Mr. Scott, agent to the Governor-General, entered into a treaty with the Singphoo chiefs. At that time the Beesa Gaum was the most intelligent and influential of the chieftains, and was publicly recognised as the agent through whom the sentiments of the British Government should be made known to the different tribes. In other respects he had no controlling authority, and was regarded by his brother chieftains as merely their equal. On the invasion of Assam by the Burmese, the Singphoos joined the force, and partook of their plunder; in fact, they had no alternative: their only option was to plunder others or to be plundered.

Prior to the conquest of Assam by the British power, the Singphoo tribes had been accustomed to make annual incursions into the province, for the purpose of obtaining slaves and plunder; but on the establishment of a British force at Suddeah, this practice was effectually restrained. From this circumstance arose their dislike to our power, which readily disposes them to listen to any adventurer who holds out to them the prospect of driving us out of the country; for with the reckless and short-sighted policy of barbarians, they never calculate the consequences of a revolt, but think that if the British troops were defeated, and our influence annihilated, all their desires would be accomplished.

The Burmese having been driven from the province, in 1824–25, by our troops, and the Singphoos completely subdued, it became necessary to adopt measures for the establishment of our future intercourse with the latter; and for this purpose, on the 3rd of May, 1826, a treaty was entered into with them, granting them terms they had no reason to expect. The following is a copy of the compact:

"Whereas we, the Singphoo chiefs named Bam, Komjoy, Meejong, Jow, Chowkhen, Jowrah, Chow, Chumun, Neenjun, Tangrang, Chowbal, Chumta, Chowrah, Chowdoo, Chowkam, Koomring, &c., are under the subjection of the British Government. We execute this agreement to Mr. David Scott, the agent to the Governor General, and hereby engage to adhere to the following terms, viz: 1st. Assam being under the sway of the British Government, we and our dependent Singphoos, who were subjects of the Assam state, acknowledge subjection to that Government. We agree not to side with the Burmese, or any other king, nor to commit any aggressions whatever; but we will obey the orders of the British Government.

"2dly. Whenever a British force may march to Assam, to protect it from foreign aggression, we will supply that force with grain, &c.; make and repair roads for it, and execute any order that may be issued to us; and we shall, on our doing so, be protected by that force.

3rd. If we abide by the terms of this agreement, no tribute shall be paid by us; but if any Assam Paicks, of their own accord, reside in our villages, the tax on such Paicks shall be paid to the British Government.

"4th. We will set at large, or cause to be liberated any Assam people whom we may have seized, and they shall have the option to reside wherever they please.

"5th. If any of the Singphoos rob any of the Assam people residing in our country, we will apprehend the former, and surrender him to the British Government; but if we fail to do so, we will make good the loss thus sustained by the latter.

"6th. We will govern and protect the Singphoos under us, as heretofore, and adjust their differences; and if any boundary dispute occur amongst us, we will not take up arms without the knowledge of the British Government.

"7th. We will adhere to the terms of this agreement, and never depart from them. This agreement shall be binding upon our brothers, sons, nephews and relatives in such way as the Agent to the Governor-General may deem proper. We have executed this agreement in the presence of many. Written at Suddeah, 5th May, 1826, A.D."

The Singphoo country remained undisturbed until the year 1830, when the invasion of Wakim Koomjoon, from the province of Hookong, on the Burmese side, took place, and was promptly repelled by Captain Neufville. On this occasion, the Luttora and Tengapanee Singphoos took part with the invader, and the Beesa Gaum with the British authorities. The assistance of the Beesa Gaum does not appear to have been of a very active nature, but his conduct was nevertheless approved by the Political Agent, and rewarded by Government. He was, however, shortly afterwards dismissed from the situation of Sunzatee, and Zalim Sing, a Soobadar of the Assam Light Infantry, who had greatly distinguished himself under Captain Neufville, was appointed to the office. Bijee Nath Sing, a Soobadar of the Assam Light Infantry, succeeded him in 1839.

In 1835, the attack of the Duffa Gaum upon the Beesa took place. This compelled the British Government to interfere for his protection, and to avenge the massacre of its subjects; but although the attacking party came from Hookong, the contest was in reality between the Khakoo Singphoos, under the Luttoora chief (who espoused the Duffa's cause), and the Now Dehing and Booree Dehing Singphoos, on the side of the Beesa; for the Duffa only brought fifty muskets with him and one hundred followers, the remainder of his force being collected within the British boundary.

The feud between the two rival chieftains, the Duffa and the Beesa, arose in 1823 A.D., two years before the assumption of the sovereignty of Assam by the British Government. A Singphoo chief of rank, named Likhee Khandoo, who had lately come over from Hookong, had proposed to the Beesa Gaum that the Singphoos, in conjunction, should attack the Bursenaputty, or chief of the Muttucks. The Beesa chief replied that he would willingly join provided the Duffa Gaum was of the party; the latter was applied to, but refused to engage in the enterprise; nevertheless the attack was made by the Singphoos, but was repulsed with severe loss to them, the Muttucks having received secret information which enabled them to prepare to receive the assailants. The prior intelligence of the attack which the Bursenaputty had received, was ascribed, whether justly or unjustly, to the Duffa chief's agency. Accordingly, in a spirit of revenge, the remaining Singphoos attacked his house, wounded his wife (who died from the effects of her wounds), and killed some of his people. It is not certain that the Beesa chief was present at this outrage, but as the party went from his house, there can be little doubt of his connivance at the transaction. After this the Duffa chief withdrew into the district of Hookong, under Burmese control; and although repeatedly invited by the British authorities to return and resume his territory, he never could be prevailed on to do so. Nor did he ever make application to obtain redress for the injuries he had sustained from the Beesa chief prior to the conquest of Assam by the British Government, and it was evidently never his intention to apply. Indeed, it would have been incompatible with Singphoo notions of honour that a chieftain should have obtained redress in this manner without retaliating upon his enemy. With this latter view, ever since his retreat from Assam, he had been gradually labouring to extend his influence amongst the Singphoos, across both the Burmese and Assam sides of the boundary line; and possessing the advantage of birth, superior connections, and a reputation for liberality, he at length succeeded in establishing an ascendancy paramount to that of the Beesa chief: which had latterly declined, owing to his connection with the British Government. The Beesa chief, and those dependent upon him, had been compelled to give up the Assamese who returned from slavery in Burmah—a measure extremely repugnant to the Singphoos, dependant as they were upon the Assamese for the means of subsistence.

Matters stood in this position up to July 1835, when the Duffa Gaum, having obtained decided influence, planned an expedition into the Beesa's territory, and appearing there unexpectedly, surprised and plundered his village, murdered his wife, his son's wife, and ninety of his people: thus retaliating in a far greater degree the injury he had sustained. On hearing of this outrage, Lieutenant Charlton ordered out a company, and instructed the Soobadar to inform the Duffa Gaum that he must forthwith quit the Assam boundary, and that, on reaching the frontier, any complaint he had to prefer against the Beesa chief would be promptly attended to. The Duffa chief refusing to comply with the mandate, Lieutenant Charlton was obliged to employ force against him; but the troops under Lieutenant Charlton's command being insufficient for the purpose, three months afterwards (in November 1835) the political agent in person moved to his assistance with two hundred and fifty men of the Assam Light Infantry.

The Duffa Gaum, anticipating an attack, had taken up a strong position in the stockades on the Menaboom hills. Prior to resorting to hostilities, every exertion was made to induce the chief to come to terms, and a three days' truce was granted for this purpose. The Khamtee chiefs and the Bursenaputtee of Muttuck, who accompanied the political agent as auxiliaries on this occasion, were required to escort the Duffa Gaum to the camp of the Political Agent as a security that his person would be respected, and that he would be permitted to return unmolested should no satisfactory result follow the meeting. The Duffa Gaum, however, being still apprehensive of treachery, could not be prevailed upon to attend the conference, until the Political Agent consented to meet him at a spot one hundred and fifty yards distant from his fort, with an escort of only a havildar and twelve soldiers. The escort having been scrupulously counted, the chief at last came out with a similar number of armed followers. His demeanour was most abject: he and his whole escort sunk down upon their knees, and taking a handful of the earth, he kissed it and said that the Company was Lord and Master thereof. He then proceeded to speak of the injuries he had sustained from the Beesa Gaum. In reply, he was told that he had no reason to complain of the British Government, as he had never represented the conduct of the Beesa chief to any of the functionaries, and that it could not be expected that the Government should take cognizance of acts which had occurred in 1823, prior to its assumption of the sovereignty of Assam. The injuries which the British Government had sustained from him were then recapitulated: the murder of its subjects, the plunder of their property, and the Duffa Gaum's stubborn persistence in retaining his position in the face of repeated injunctions that he should withdraw from the territory within the Assam boundary. It was further brought to his recollection that the British Government had repeatedly offered him repossession of his territory, provided he came in a peaceable manner, but that it was incompatible with its dignity to allow him to attempt to extort by force that which had been given spontaneously. He was then required, First, to make good, by an annual instalment in money, elephants' teeth, or gold dust, the loss of 8000 rupees that our merchants had sustained by his treacherous attack on Beesa: furnishing security, or a hostage, for the fulfilment of his engagement; and, Secondly, to dismiss the auxiliary Singphoos whom he had brought from the Burmese territory: and as a security for their not returning he was to give up their arms. The Duffa Gaum agreed to both these propositions, apparently in the most joyful manner, and promised faithfully to come in the following morning; but the next day he sent a letter into camp referring entirely to his ancient dispute with the Beesa chief, and making no allusion whatever to the terms proposed to him. Upon this, the British force took up a position within five hundred yards of his stockade; but the Duffa Gaum's agent immediately came out and said, that if the Political Agent would advance alone to a place within one hundred and fifty yards of the fort, the chief would come out and accompany him to camp. The Political Agent complied with the request, remained at the appointed spot half an hour at considerable personal risk, and called upon the Duffa Gaum to fulfil to his promise. The answer given was, that the Duffa Gaum had no confidence in the sincerity of the Political Agent, as Wakutchangnang had sent him a flint, powder and ball, the evening before: which was equivalent to an intimation that his intentions were warlike whilst proposing peace. The Agent urged in the strongest manner that no such message had been sent; but finding the Duffa Gaum immovable, hostilities were reluctantly resorted to. A signal was given to the battery, and the fire commenced; the stockade was carried, and the Duffa chief fled beyond the frontier.

Not the slightest doubt was entertained of the individual desire of the Duffa chief for peace; but the Khamtee chiefs, being irritated by certain proposed innovations in 1834—such as taking a census and taxing them—were the first, it is believed, to call in the Duffa chief, with a view of exciting troubles and obstructing the maturity of our plans; and thus was the negotiation marred.

In the year 1838 public tranquillity was again disturbed by a feud between the Peshee and Let chiefs, which compelled the British Government to interfere and punish the former: who, contrary to his agreement, persisted in attacking the latter. The Luttora chief likewise violated his compact, by giving aid to the Peshee chief, and was driven from the Company's territory.

Though the Tengapanee Singphoos did not arrive in time to join in a body with the Khamtee chiefs, in the attack made on the post of Suddeah in January 1839, their disaffection was apparent in their unprovoked attack upon, and plunder of, the villages in the Saikwah district, when they carried off many Dooaneahs. In consequence of this outrage, a detachment of troops visited in November 1839, the principal villages of Inshaw, Dobom, Inban, Luttora, Koomkie, and Tang Sang Tang; situated at the foot of the Mishmee hills, between the Kerempanee north, and Mena Boom hills south, in the vicinity of the Tengapanee, which takes its rise in the Mena Boom hills south. On this occasion the whole of the chiefs were assembled, and the heinousness of their late conduct explained: fines were imposed in proportion to their means, and their submission and pledges required to an extent never before obtained, besides the restitution of most of the Dooaneahs carried away from Saikwah. The confederacy between the Singphoos and Kamtees was broken up, and the expulsion of the Deerack Tawah Gohain effected, with the loss of his village and a quantity of grain.

In November 1841, considerable alarm pervaded the north-east frontier, owing to a report that the Tippum Rajah, aided by the Burmese and Singphoos from both sides of the border, meditated an incursion into Assam. To remove this impression, a tour was made by the Political Agent with a company of the Assam Light Infantry, a body of Golundaz, and two three pounders carried on elephants, through the greater portion of the Singphoo territory. The route pursued was from Saikwah up the Burrampooter river to the Tengapanee; and on passing the villages of Kinglong, Dohing Koomkee, the principal chiefs, Neesaka of Jusha, Ong of Luttora, Labing of Dobom, Tang Sang Tang, Koomong of Koomkee, and Samnong, son of the Wakhet chief, paid their respects. From thence the party proceeded up the bed of the Tengapanee, by the site of the former village of Luttora, on to Naing and Meerappanee, and commenced the ascent over the Mena Boom hills: a most trying undertaking for elephants, as they had to travel along a narrow ridge in some places only a few paces wide, and entirely composed of loose stones; the sides frequently presenting dangerous precipices. It was in descending this ridge that the laden elephants encountered the greatest difficulty; yet they managed to get down without the necessity of dismounting the guns, and reached Beesa and Ningroo in perfect safety. The Singphoos thus learned the folly of trusting to their stockades in their fastnesses, when guns could be brought against them by moderate exertion and ingenuity. It was hoped that this tour would also tend to repress the feuds so constantly arising amongst themselves; seeing that justice could be administered even in retreats the most secluded and difficult of access. But this expectation was not realized; for in the year 1842 the Tippum Rajah (brother of Jegessur Sing, the last rajah of Assam, said to be now governor of Hookong and Mogong) sent the Beesa chief six pounds of needles, half of which were broken, to be distributed by him amongst the Singphoos: a token or signal of alliance and preparation for war. This intimation was followed up in January 1843 by an attack on a party consisting of one Jemadar, one Havildar, one Naick, and twenty Sipahees located in a small stockade at Beesa. Some previous altercation had occurred between the Jemadar and the Beesa chief regarding the repair of the stockade, which not having been effected, the Jemadar had contemptuously called the Beesa chief an old cow, and in return vengeance was vowed in intelligible terms. After holding out for some days, three Sipahees being killed and three wounded in the defence, the Jemadar was unfortunately induced to surrender himself and party prisoners of war; the treacherous Singphoos having assured him that the posts of Ningroo and Koojoo had fallen into their hands, and our troops been totally defeated. Trusting to their mercy and honour, he caused his men to cease firing; and oaths were freely taken in support of promises of good and honourable treatment; but the instant the Singphoos gained admittance into the stockade, the Jemadar and the whole party were disarmed and bound. The next morning the Jemadar and Havildar were led out by the Singphoos and tied up to a tree, and fired at; after this they were hewn to pieces with a short sword, on the same spot where one of the Singphoos had been shot by the Jemadar when in possession of the stockade. Nine of the Sipahees were sold into slavery, some to Hookong and Burkhamtee. Thus signally did the Singphoos gratify their revenge, at the commencement of the irruption or attempt to break through the line of outposts and lay waste the whole country.

Their second and third attacks on the Koojoo and Ningroo stockades, defended by European officers, were completely frustrated. The Koojoo stockade was besieged for some days, but a sally being made on the enemy whilst the Singphoos were at dinner, they were defeated and fled in the utmost consternation. The Ningroo stockade was likewise at night suddenly attacked and taken by surprise, but after a short, sharp struggle, in which several lives were lost, the Singphoos left the stockade in greater haste than they entered it.

The Tippum Rajah's sister was married to the late king of Ava, and she is supposed to be in favour with the present king. It may be owing to her influence that the Tippum Rajah is reported to be now Governor of Hookong, to take advantage of any opportunity to invade Assam. Scarcely a year passes without some such reports being spread throughout the province, and there is great reason to believe that the Singphoo insurrection of 1843 was raised at the suggestion, or at least through the connivance of the Rajah; as many Burmese or Shans under his jurisdiction crossed the frontier and joined the insurgents in the hope of plundering the province. Had success attended their first attempts, it cannot be doubted but that many more would have soon followed their example, in the speedy removal of slaves and property from Assam. But the real origin of the insurrection was the occupation of the Koojoo tea garden and other tea tracts. The constant desertion of the Dooaneah slaves and dependants, who are the people chiefly employed in cultivation under the Singphoos, besides the advance of civilization consequent on the establishment of a considerable village at Jeypore with European residents, was the source of much heart-burning. The occupation of Muttuck, formerly under native management, must also have proved distasteful to a savage people possessing a wild country and delighting in extensive hunting-grounds. These circumstances, aggravated by frequent quarrels with the Sipahees at Ningroo, the unauthorized apprehension of two Let Singphoos by the Jemadar, and a desire of revenge for the execution, many years ago, of Ningroola Gaum's kinsman, certainly contributed to produce the insurrection of 1843.

Viewing the nature of our connection with the Singphoos generally, it must be acknowledged that the balance of advantage had been decidedly in their favour; for while we have been called upon to fight their battles, little or no assistance has, comparatively, been afforded us by them. Being a rude, treacherous people, little faith can be placed in them; neither can we expect they will be influenced or bound by any treaties not in accordance with their own views: in fact they have in no respect fulfilled their obligations to the British Government.

The Singphoo country is eminently unfavourable to the operations of regular troops, owing to its mountainous character, unrelieved by plains or table lands, the want of roads, the extreme scarcity of provisions, the absence of local means of transport, and above all the unhealthiness of the climate. The Government is likewise put to a great expense without commensurate benefit, for in such a rude and barbarous state of society revenue cannot be collected without the employment of military force; and this is not always adequate to the success of hostile operations, because of its paucity and the advantage afforded to the natives by the natural defences of the country: of which they are not slow to avail themselves.

In reviewing the different tribes of Assam, it may not be out of place to offer a brief sketch of one or two of the chieftains.

Wakut-chang-nang is the son of a Singphoo chief who submitted to Captain Neufville in 1825, and received a present of a gun and other articles from him, which he requited by firing upon the captain a day or two afterwards. The ball missed Captain Neufville and went through Lieutenant Kerr's hat without doing him any injury. Subsequent to this, Wakut-chang-nang absconded to Hookong within the Burmese boundary, and only returned in 1835 to the Assam territory. During his sojourn within the Hookong territory he is stated to have committed several murders; and with the money accumulated by crime and robbery, he has been enabled to marry the Beesa Gaum's daughter. From his having been the principal agent in breaking off the negotiation with the Duffa chief, and consequently the cause of the subsequent bloodshed, he was imprisoned during 1836–37 at Bishnath. He is now residing at Beesa, and is considered, as heretofore, an intriguing, dangerous character. The Beesa Gaum, having been implicated in the rebellion of 1843, is now a state prisoner for life; he is nearly blind, and his career may be said to have closed, as it is not probable he will survive many years. He was supposed to be a man of good sense and to possess considerable information regarding border politics, but of no enlarged capacity or superior energy of character, and totally incapable of forming those comprehensive designs which have been attributed to him. He is not of a warlike character. Most of his battles have been fought by others: for a Singphoo chief is not expected to head his troops in action. Nevertheless his disposition is sanguinary, and it is said his career has been marked by blood and treachery in a greater degree than usual, even amongst the Singphoos.

The Shan is the written character used by the Singphoos, and their language is distinct from any of the neighbouring tribes: they write on leaves and a peculiar kind of paper. As yet no European has sufficiently studied the language to appreciate justly the Singphoo literature, or to prepare elementary works for the guidance of others. Nor are we aware of there being any written works in the language either historical or theological. As civil members of society they are anything but good subjects, from their excessive laziness, immoderate addiction to opium, and general uncertainty of character. They are so indolent and improvident, that notwithstanding they have the most fertile soil in Assam, which yields fruit with little labour, and might be made to produce an abundant crop—notwithstanding, too, their freedom from taxation, grain is always so extravagantly dear, that during several months in the year the people are reduced to subsist on yams and other roots found in the jungles. Almost the whole of the field work is performed by the women and slaves, while the men delight in lounging about the villages, and basking in the sun, when not engaged in hunting or war.

The religion of the Singphoos appears to be a mixture of all the various idolatries and superstitions of the natives with whom they have intercourse. They seem to have no fixed principles common to the whole tribe. Their ostensible worship is that of Guduma, whose temples and priests are to be found in all their principal villages. They are also in the habit of deifying any Singphoos who may chance to be killed in action during a foray upon some other tribe or village, and of sacrificing to them as to their penates. On emergencies, such as famine, pestilence, or danger, they make offerings to the "Ning Deota," God of the Elements, called also "Ningschees;" sacrificing buffaloes, hogs, and cocks. The skulls of the buffaloes so offered are afterwards hung up in their houses as mementos of their own piety.

Their funeral ceremonies are simple. The poorer classes burn or bury the body, according to the previously expressed wish of the deceased, and invariably make to the deity an offering of a pig, fowl, or fish, through their Deodhies or priests. On the death of a chief, numerous ceremonies are performed: the body is detained until all the friends of the deceased can be assembled, when buffaloes, pigs, and deer are sacrificed, a grand feast is given, and spirituous liquor distributed to the company. The corpse is then committed to the earth, the priest chants a prayer for the deceased, a clay tomb is raised over the remains, and the grave is encircled with a bamboo fence. Sacrifices are always offered up on the death of every Singphoo, according to the means of the surviving relatives; no matter whether death be caused by accident or war, or in the course of nature.

Polygamy, without restriction, prevails among the Singphoos, and they make no distinction between the children born of Singphoo women and those born of foreign or Assamese women. They reject with horror the idea of infanticide, under any shape or pretext. Marriage is only forbidden with a mother or sister: they may marry stepmothers, brothers' widows, or any other relative. In the marriage ceremony the bridegroom has to present the parents of the bride with a Khamtee Dhao, or short sword, a velvet jacket, a silk Dhota, and a slave; the rich give gold and silver, buffaloes, and as many slaves as the wealth of the bridegroom will permit. The bridegroom has also to furnish a marriage feast to the friends and relations of the bride; and after the Deodhies or priests have performed a certain religious ceremony, the bride is delivered over to the bridegroom, and the jewels,

&c., which are on her person, are returned to her parents.

If a man commits adultery, he is obliged to pay damages according to the demand of the injured husband, in slaves, buffaloes, dhoties, swords, money, or beads; and if he cannot pay the damages, he pays the penalty of his crime in confinement. No damages are demanded for the violation of an unmarried woman or virgin; but in the event of her being found pregnant, the ravisher has to give the parents three slaves and one buffalo, and the issue is claimed by the man. It is optional with himself to marry his victim, or not. Theft is punished by exacting from the thief double the value of the property stolen.

The Singphoos entertain strange ideas of honour and revenge. Compatibly with their customs and rude notions of religion, a Singphoo chief could not ever abandon, without dishonour, the application of the *lex talionis* to one who had murdered his relative; although, from circumstances of policy, or deficiency of means, he might postpone the gratification of his vengeance to an indefinite period. A mistaken feeling of religion, combined with private affection for the deceased, fully accounts for this perverted state of mind. The Singphoos imagine that the soul of the murdered individual will torment them until his manes are appeased by the death of one of his enemies; and further, that the anger of their deity would be roused should an opportunity of retaliation be neglected. Nor is the retribution to be limited to the actual perpetrator of the homicide. If death be occasioned by violence committed, or supposed to be committed by any one, the relations are never appeased until they have murdered one of the family to which the murderer belonged. An innocent person is thus often murdered, who is quite ignorant of the injury committed by his tribe or family.

The houses of the Singphoos are generally nothing but long sheds, roofed in with grass or bamboo leaves, and the walls composed of split bamboo. The floor of the dwelling part is raised about four feet from the ground; and the entrance forms an extensive porch, in which are congregated pigs, fowls, household and agricultural implements, and where women may generally be seen pounding rice. These buildings are sometimes one hundred feet long, and divided into compartments allotted to several families. Occasionally immense houses may be seen, which are occupied by powerful chiefs; the timbers of these buildings being of such enormous size and length as to render it a matter of surprise that they could have been erected by mere manual labour. At the burning of the Ningrang chief's house, when the village was surprised by our troops in 1843, the officers remarked that the posts were of prodigious diameter and length; and it was regretted that war rendered it necessary to destroy such a magnificent residence. The mansion was entered by a flight of several steps leading up to the floor, and was divided into numerous rooms by partitions of split bamboo.

The Singphoos have nothing approaching to what we call government: each chief is independent, collecting no revenue, nor directing in person any force, although he may influence the movements of others. The Singphoos are of a tawny complexion, and a cunning expression, with long bodies and short legs. They are implacable, cruel, and treacherous; stealing upon and murdering with the short sword at night those who have offended or injured them; and are ever ready to coalesce for a foray, if there is a prospect of success. Casualties that occur from the contentions of one tribe with another, murders resulting from private jealousy, the difficulty of procuring food, and exposure to the inclemency of the weather, help to keep the population scanty all over the north-east frontier. In fact, the great cause of the thinness of the population is the want of food, arising from the absence of productive industry. The unsettled and lawless state of society among the Burmese and Singphoos appears likewise to operate in retarding the extension of trade; and this evil cannot be rectified until these tribes are brought more completely under subjection to the British Government. That once effected, a mart might be formed at our extreme boundary; though the scantiness of the population in these regions would probably for some time prevent the establishment of a very brisk trade.

Hookoom is distant from Suddeah about 200 miles; a miserable, desolate, backward country intervening: in fact, almost an entire jungle throughout. At Moonkoom there would be a larger field for commerce, as water communication by the Irawaddy is facile. Broad cloths, &c., could probably be conveyed thither cheaper, viâ Rangoon, than from the Burrampooter. The same obstacles exist to opening a trade between Assam and the provinces of Yunan, owing to the greater proximity of Yunan to the Burmese empire. By all accounts a considerable trade is carried on between the two countries, viâ Bamow: a Burmese town within twenty miles of the confines of Yunan; and from the facility of transport which the Irawaddy affords, we may infer that British goods could be supplied at a cheaper rate, and with greater safety, from Rangoon or from Moulmein through the Sangha, than could be effected from Assam. The poverty of the people on this part of our frontier is such that scarcely any one can afford to buy woollens, excepting the chiefs, and even those persons generally receive them as presents from the officers of Government. It would therefore be desirable to send up articles of less value. The articles chiefly in demand are salt, cloths, tobacco, opium, knives, needles, cups and saucers, basons and plates.

In 1828, by way of experiment, and to test the possibility of reviving trade, a Government investment of woollen goods to the amount of 4000 rupees, was sent up to Suddeah; but it actually took eight years before the whole stock was sold off, and it would not then, probably, have been disposed of, had not the price been reduced thirty per cent. below prime cost. It was sold during the first and second years of its appearance in the market, at prime cost; afterwards at a reduction of ten, twenty, and thirty per cent. Since then, a trade, such as it is, has been established at Suddeah by native merchants, at considerable risk; for the Government will not undertake to give compensation for any losses the traders may sustain, either from sudden attacks, or in their transactions with these wild tribes. Notwithstanding the apparently hopeless prospect of any immediate commercial intercourse taking place between Assam and any portion of western China, there can be no doubt that as civilization advances, the intervening tracts will be traversed, and a lucrative trade may then connect districts now separated by dense forests.

It remains only to mention that, some difference of opinion existing as to the boundary line between Assam and the Burmese territory, it was deemed expedient to define the limits of both countries by a special mission to the disputed point; and for this purpose, in 1837, Dr. Bayfield was deputed to proceed from Ava and join the Burmese Governor of Mogaum, and in the presence of Major White, Political Agent of Upper Assam, to settle the question. Major White, accompanied by Dr. Griffiths, Captain Hannay, and Lieut. Bigge, and the neighbouring native chiefs, with ninety followers, accordingly set out from Namroop Pathar, on the 19th February; and on the 25th of the same month they reached Yaoung Sang Nullah, on the north face of the Patkoe boundary, or range, where the Burmese governor had agreed that the conference should take place.

In this dreary wilderness of hills and jungle, the impossibility of obtaining an adequate supply of provisions for ninety persons (the commissariat being carried from the plains of Assam) presented an insuperable obstacle to the prolonged stay of the party with Major White. Having therefore waited till the 5th March, daily expecting the arrival of the Burmese Governor and Dr. Bayfield; and the whole of their provisions being consumed, with the exception of a bare sufficiency for the wants of the party on their return, the Major was constrained to retrace his steps to Suddeah. Captain Hannay, however, pushed on unencumbered, in company with Dr. Griffiths (deputed for scientific purposes to Ava), hoping to meet the Burmese Governor and accomplish the object of the mission: which he did.

On the 9th March, Captain Hannay and Dr. Bayfield pointed out to the Burmese Governor of Mogaum the boundary line on the summit of the Patkoe Mountains, and read to him an extract of the treaty between the Rajahs of Mogaum and Assam, establishing the boundary in 1323, A.S., or 1402, A.D. The purport of this extract was that, in the year 1145, A.S., equivalent to 1224 of the Christian era, Sookhapah, the founder of the Ahoom Dynasty, having taken his departure from Moonkhoom, invaded Assam; and, taking possession of the country on the other side of the Patkoe range, he established Khanjang, or Nunyangpanee, as the boundary: appointing the Bor Gohain to the government of the district, and directing that the customary tribute should be remitted to him in Assam. This settlement continued until the year 1323, equivalent to 1402, A.D., during the reign of Soodangpha, the eighth Rajah of the Ahoon dynasty; when a brother of his, named Towsoolie, having quarrelled with him, went to Moonkhoom and instigated the Rajah to invade Assam. The attack being, however, repulsed, an accommodation afterwards took place between the two Rajahs, and the Patkoe range of hills was established as the boundary. On this occasion a stone image was put up to indicate the limits; and both the Rajahs, dipping their hands in the water, vowed personal friendship, and swore reciprocally to respect each other's territory. This compact remained unviolated for a period of 400 years up to the period when the Burmese invaded Assam.

MUTTUCKS.

MUTTUCKS: their origin and religion—Severely persecuted by Seba Sing—Revolt under Luckme Sing—Get possession of the capital, and make Luckme Sing and all his court prisoners—Ramakant Bor Deka ascends the throne—Re-action in favour of Luckme Sing, who is restored—Barbarous punishment inflicted on Ramakant Bor Deka, his brother, and father—General massacre of the Muttuck chiefs and their followers—Rebellion of the Moa Mareyas—Expulsion of Rajah Goureenath, who solicits the assistance of the British Government—Captain Welsh sent with one or two battalions—Replaces Goureenath on the throne—Rajah Kumalepur invades Muttuck, but unable to obtain permanent possession—British Government annexes the whole of Muttuck to the district of Luckimpoor—Husbandry the chief occupation of the Muttucks—Tea plant indigenous—Exertions of Major Jenkins in promoting its cultivation

The Muttucks were originally a rude tribe settled in a district called Mooran or Muttuck, who prior to the Ahoom invasion of 1224, A.D., had learned the doctrines of the Hindoo religion from two Gosains named respectively Madho Deo, and Sunkur Deo. The Gosains were followers of Krishen, and their doctrine particularly differed from that of the other Hindoos of Assam, in their refusing to worship the images of Doorga. The appellation of Moa Mureyas arose from its being the name of the place where a Shuster was founded, and from which the doctrines of the Muttucks emanated. They were allowed to exercise their religion unmolested, until the reign of Seba Sing, between 1714 and 1744, A.D.; when, animated by a spirit of sectarian zeal, the Queen, Phoolsuree, inflicted a sore wound upon their religious feelings by compelling them to worship the images of Doorga, and to put the distinguishing marks of the followers of that deity on their foreheads. But persecution, as usual, failed in checking this sectarian spirit; and the numbers of the Muttucks having greatly increased in the reign of Luckmi Sing, 1769, A.D., they revolted from his authority. The immediate cause of the first insurrection is attributable to two circumstances,—a bigoted religious persecution, and a haughty, inconsiderate, oppressive demeanour towards the Muttuck chiefs, and their adherents.

Soon after the succession of Luckmi Sing to the throne of his brother, Rajeswur Sing, Rajhan Mooran, a Muttuck chief, was commissioned to procure a thousand elephants for Luckmi Sing, who was a great admirer of these animals. The chief obeyed, and from time to time he presented many elephants to the king. On one occasion, having been unusually fortunate in capturing two hundred and fifty elephants, he took them to the capital to show them to his Majesty; but as it was customary to apprize the Bor Borowa of his intended visit, that the circumstance might be previously announced to the King, he was proceeding to the residence of that functionary, when he met the Bor Borowa's son going on business to the King. Unfortunately he was persuaded to accompany the young man, unmindful of the indiscretion of deviating from the established rules of respect and courtesy to the Bor Borowa.

On Rajhan's arrival at the palace, the King ordered his servants to prepare to attend him during the inspection of the elephants. The Bor Borowa being obliged to be present on all such occasions, and hearing that Rajhan Mooran had ventured to approach the Rajah without the usual formality of an introduction, determined to wreak his vengeance on the insolent Muttuck. Luckmi Sing inspected the elephants, and was highly pleased with Rajhan Mooran's promptitude and assiduity in the execution of his orders. He warmly expressed his royal approbation of the conduct of the chief, and, handsomely rewarding him, retired to the palace.

The Bor Borowa now took the opportunity of sending for Rajhan Mooran to learn his reasons for not having apprized him of his arrival before he had sought an interview with the king. The excuse pleaded by Rajhan Mooran was unheeded; the Bor Borowa was implacable, and directed the infliction of a severe corporal punishment with the cane. So strictly was this order executed, that Rajhan Mooran was cast into the road in a lifeless state. Here he was recognised by his countrymen, and conveyed away; and with good treatment, but not without difficulty, he recovered.

The undeserved insult and chastisement he had received from the Bor Borowa, however, rankled deeply in his breast; and he lost no time, when able to move, in proceeding to the Muttuck Gosain Ushtobhoj,[2] to claim his intercession in obtaining redress for the insufferable dishonour he had been subjected to.

The Moa Mureya Gosain Ushtobhoj, commiserating the ill-treatment Rajhan Mooran had met with, resolved, a short time afterwards, on visiting the Rajah to obtain reparation. He accordingly set out with his Bhukuts, or religious disciples, and meeting the Rajah's fleet on the river, he paid his respects to the Rajah, contrary to the wishes of the Bor Borowa Keerteerchund, Prime Minister. This conduct greatly incensed the Bor Borowa, who immediately sent for the Gosain and treated him with great harshness and abuse, for the temerity he had evinced in presuming to visit the Rajah without being announced by himself. The Bhukuts who had accompanied him to the interview were likewise ill-treated This indig-

[2] The name of the Moa Mareya Muttuck Gosain is Nahor; he is called Ushtobhoj, the eight handed priest, or an incarnation of the Deity: a title which he assumed in order to receive greater adoration from the people. He established his claim to the title by a device or deception. Making three men stand behind him, from under a covering they presented their hands in front of his body, and these, with his own, made his credulous disciples believe he really had eight hands. Having also some defect in his legs, he was known by the appellation of the Lame Moa Mareya Priest Nahor.

nity highly offended the Gosain, and he determined to take an early opportunity of retaliating the outrage. With this view, he took measures for ascertaining the number of disciples and adherents he might rely on, and found, to his satisfaction, that the census returned one hundred thousand persons.

The feelings of the Muttucks being now exasperated to the highest degree by the degradations and insults to which they were subjected by the Assam nobles; the present appeared to them a fitting opportunity to rise and avenge their wrongs. The Bor Deka, son of the Muttuck Gosain, having long entertained ambitious views, encouraged Rajhan Mooran to assemble all the Muttuck chiefs and followers willing to co-operate with them; expressing his belief that with their united forces, success would attend their efforts. In the mean time he remained quiet, the better to conceal his designs, and commenced building a large mound near Jorehath, on which he intimated his intention to found a Shuster, to be denominated the Bor Bhatee. Each man who was willing to join in the insurrection was enjoined to bring in one hand a lump of earth and in the other a reed. By this device the Bor Deka's designs passed unobserved, and a multitude of followers were ascertained to be ripe for the approaching contest.

Mohun Bor Jona Gohain, eldest brother of Luckmi Sing, being marked with the smallpox, and a slit in the ear, was, by the Assamese customs, disqualified from ascending the throne. Notwithstanding this, however, with a view of concealing their real designs, the Muttucks proposed to the prince to join the insurrectionary force; promising to place him on the throne in the event of the success of the insurrection. Tempted by the promise, the prince joined the rebels, who immediately marched towards the capital at Rungpore, on the banks of the Dikho river. Luckme Sing having been informed of the movement, ordered the Assam chiefs to proceed and punish the insolent Muttucks, and bring him the ringleaders of the insurrection. The rival forces met near the Thowra Dole Temple, on the banks of the Dehing river, and after a slight skirmish, in which their commander, the Doabyah Phokun, was killed, the Assamese were defeated, and fled. Bhectorial Phokun then succeeded to the command, and perceiving that Mohun Bor Jona Gohain, the elder brother of the reigning king was at the head of the rebel force, not only refused to oppose the prince and the invaders, but went and paid homage to the Gosain. The Muttucks, thus meeting with no opposition, marched in and took possession of the capital; and with such promptitude that Rajah Luckme Sing and all his court were taken prisoners. Luckme Sing was then incarcerated and harshly treated: food scarcely sufficient for his subsistence being allowed him. The Bor Borowa Keerteerchund was seized and put to death, with all his family, relations, and friends; and many nobles also shared the same fate.

Ramakant Bor Deka now took possession of the throne, and Rajhan Mooran became Bor Borowa; while the prince, Bor Jona Gohain, who thus traitorously acted against his family and country, was put off with the plea that he was incapacitated to reign as king by reason of the personal mutilation already adverted to.

A few months after this, a reaction took place. The Assamese hearing of the indignities their king had suffered, and that Chunder Deka, a younger brother of the Bor Deka, had actually struck the king three blows with a cane for sitting in his presence when he visited him in his confinement, they determined on expelling the Muttucks from their country, either by force or stratagem. Numerous chiefs and others readily entered into the spirit of the conspiracy. A grand fete was to be given at the Bihoo festival in March 1769–70 A.D.; Rajhan Mooran and the Muttuck chiefs were to be invited; and the Assamese were to attend with arms concealed under their dress. Mogolee Jiekee Muneeporee,[3] Queen both of Rajeswar Sing and Luckme Sing, whom Rajhan Mooran had taken unto himself, was to preside and be the principal agent in the accomplishment of the project. She was to persuade Rajhan Mooran to accompany her to the dance, and when there, she was, if possible by some subterfuge, to obtain possession of his sword, which he constantly wore; and if his attention could be attracted to the dance she was to cut him down, which would be the signal for the Assamese to fall upon and slaughter the Muttucks. This diabolical plot, from the unanimity and secresy of the conspirators, was executed with the most perfect success. The Queen, who had obtained considerable influence over Rajhan Mooran, without difficulty induced him to place his sword in her hand, that he might, as she said, more easily arrange his dress, which she had artfully managed somewhat to displace. While in the act of stooping down, the Queen dexterously stepped behind him, and with one blow on the hinder part of the thigh completely disabled him. The conspirators, anxiously expecting the signal, instantly came up and put an end to his existence. The Assamese then fell on the remaining unarmed Muttucks, and a dreadful massacre ensued.

The conspirators, having successfully carried through their plot against Rajhan Mooran and the principal Muttuck chief, proceeded to the residence of the Bor Deka Ramakant, the usurper; his father, brothers, women, and children, were, with all the principal parties, captured; but Ramakant, on hearing of the death of Rajhan Mooran, had made his escape from the capital. He was, however, seized near Bet-barree and brought back to pay the forfeit of his ambition and rebellion. Luckme Sing was immediately released from imprisonment and again placed on his throne. The first order issued by the king after his restoration, was for the extermination of the Muttucks. The usurper Ramakant Bor Deka, and his brother Chunder Deka, as well as the Muttuck Gosain their father, were tied to the legs of fierce, newly caught elephants, and ignominiously dragged round the city, assailed with mud and filth and every kind of indignity that an infuriated, relentless mob, intoxicated with triumph, could inflict; and to close the scene they suffered the cruel and disgraceful death of impalement. The Muttuck chiefs and their followers were everywhere hunted down like wild beasts, and put to death: neither men, women, nor children were spared. In fact, such was the animosity of the Assamese against the Muttucks, for the time, that they seemed bereft of all feelings of mercy or compassion. Vast numbers of the Muttucks died of hunger in the jungles, and an incalculable number perished by the sword of the insatiate populace.

Luckme Sing, being now under no farther apprehensions for the safety of him-

[3] This princess was the daughter of the Munepore Rajah; she was first married to Rajeswur Sing, and afterwards to his brother, Luckme Sing. The Muneepories are called Mogolies, and a tank, temple and an estate is to this day called the Mogolie Princess's Pokhuree and Khat. In the Assam annals, she is called Koorung Neyune.

self or throne, richly rewarded the actors in the late tragedy with rank and wealth: and thus terminated the first rebellion of the Muttucks.

In 1784 the Moa Mareyas again rebelled, and having expelled the Rajah Goureenath they proceeded to place two others upon the Guddee, or throne, one named Bhurt Sing as Rajah of Rungpore or Upper Assam, the other Surbamend (the father of Malebar Bursenaputtee, who died in 1839) as Rajah of Mooran or Muttuck. Both these chiefs marked their rule by establishing a mint, and some of their coins are to be met with at the present day. Being driven from Upper Assam, the Rajah Goureenath solicited the aid of the British Government; and his request being acceded to, Captain Welsh was sent with one or two battalions, in 1794, A.D. Having taken Rungpore, Goureenath was replaced on the Guddee; but Captain Welsh did not penetrate into the Muttuck country. The next Rajah, Kumalepur, raised two corps of Hindoostanees, armed and disciplined in the English fashion, and ordered them to undertake the conquest of Muttuck; but although successful in some degree, they were unable to obtain permanent possession, owing to the harassing mode of warfare pursued by the Bursenaputtee, who retired to his fastnesses. However, the struggle was at length terminated by his agreeing to pay an annual tribute in the shape of elephants, Moongah silk, &c. It is asserted by the Assamese at Rungpore and Jorehath that, at this period, the Bursenaputtee agreed to pay a tribute of 10,000 rupees; but that chief positively denied this to the Political Agent, and it is believed there is no record in existence of such a sum, or even part of it, being paid: though the acknowledgment of the Rajah of Assam is undeniable. As regards the Muttucks, the statements of the people connected with the late Court of Assam, and the followers of Doorga throughout the province, ought to be received with a great deal of caution; for both classes are animated by a bitter spirit of hatred, occasioned by the twofold conquest and plunder of their capital; and the temporary triumph of a rival sectarian party still rankles in their minds.

It is difficult to ascertain what was the precise status of the Bursenaputtee in the distracted reigns of Chunderkant and Poorunder Sing. It is said that the usual tribute was paid, but this is denied by the other party; we presume, therefore, that in these weak and divided times the Muttucks were nearly independent. When the Burmese invaded the country, the Bursenaputtee, at their requisition, afforded them supplies in labour and provisions, but no aid in troops or money; and they, therefore, made no attempt to seize his possessions. On the conquest of Assam by the British Government, the Bursenaputtee acknowledged its supremacy, and bound himself to obey its orders; he further engaged to supply three hundred soldiers in time of war, no tribute having been demanded of him. The interior management of his territory was left in his own hands, excepting as regarded cases of murder and other capital offences, which were to be made over for trial to the Agent of the Governor-General or Political Agent in Upper Assam. This arrangement had evidently in view the impressing a rude people with a greater regard for human life, which the more rigid investigation and sanctity of British forms of justice might be expected to create. This state of things subsisted until January 1835, when, under the instructions of the Agent to the Governor-General, the obligation to supply troops was commuted into an annual payment of 1800 rupees.

No census has been taken of the population, but from the best information it is estimated at sixty thousand or seventy thousand persons. It yields a revenue of 20,000 rupees per annum.

In his personal manners the late Bursenaputtee Malebur was plain and straightforward, and accustomed to think and act for himself. In his political character, his fidelity was much doubted a few years back, but he was always found ready to answer every call; as evinced in the expedition against the Duffa Guam in 1835, and the Singphoo Luttora chief in 1838, which proved that he was faithful to his engagement. But his communications with British officers were not always carried on in the smoothest manner. Accustomed to act as an independent chief for forty or fifty years, and his territory being unoccupied by troops, either Burmese or British, he was naturally independent and blunt in his manners; which bearing, combining with the testiness of age and dislike of innovation natural to that period of life, occasionally gave rise to improprieties of expression and seeming acts of disobedience. He departed this life in January 1839, leaving ten sons, five daughters, and three widows; and, pending the final orders of Government, Muttuck was placed under Bhageerut Majoo Gohain, the second son of the late chief: the Bor Gohain, or eldest son, having waved his claim of birth in compliance with the wishes of his father.

On the 4th of August 1839, the Political Agent was directed to confer on the Majoo Gohain the title of Bursenaputtee, and the management of Lower Muttuck, on his agreeing to the conditions offered for his acceptance. These were based on the settlement entered into with his late father, but a new census was required to determine the amount of tribute to be paid. These terms also withheld Upper Muttuck, until an amicable understanding could be come to between the chiefs of that part of the country; who, with their spiritual head, the Tiphook Muhunt, were averse to the rule of the family of the late chief. This party being only 1000, or 1500, out of a population of 60,000, it seemed hard to sever them from the jurisdiction of the Bursenaputtee, without any specific acts of oppression having been committed by the late chief or his family. The real objection rested on religious grounds: they are the disciples of a Gosain or priest professing different religious tenets from those of the Bursenaputtee's family; consequently they preferred a ruler of their own persuasion, although they had not experienced any persecution from the late Bursenaputtee.

In November 1839, the Political Agent arrived at Rungagora, the capital of Muttuck, and having assembled the principal members of the late chief's family, and head men of the district, made known to them the resolution of Government. The Majoo Gohain Bhagerut and his brothers, finding that Upper Muttuck was not at once to be included in the settlement, peremptorily refused to accept of the management of the country; the whole of Muttuck was therefore annexed to the district of Luckimpoor, and pensions in money and land, to the amount of 7637 rupees per annum, were granted for the support of the members of the late chief's family.

Thus terminated the independence of the Muttucks, a rude, fanatical, stiff-necked people. Accustomed to a very slight assessment, tendered to their chief in the shape of presents for settling their disputes, and exercising a considerable share in their own government, it was feared they would not readily submit to the heavier rate of taxation for the purposes of good government under British rule; but these apprehensions, it seems, were unfounded, since, for the last four years, no resort to force has been found necessary to compel taxation, or to further any other measures for their general welfare.

Husbandry is the chief occupation of the Muttucks; and their district possessing a fine fertile soil and abounding in extensive rice plains, intersected by large tracts of tree and grass jungle, expectations are entertained that, in the course of time, this country will prove a prosperous and valuable acquisition; if improvements are not impeded by the inroads of border tribes. Two corps of local Assam Light Infantry, and a company of local Artillery are ever vigilantly occupied in promptly suppressing combinations or insurrections raised with a view to the acquisition of plunder and slaves from our subjects; and there is, therefore, little fear of any organized obstruction to improvement.

The tea plant is indigenous in Muttuck, and the Assam Tea Company have cultivated many gardens, greatly to the benefit of Upper Assam; and if the company steadily prosecute the speculation, thousands of labourers will, in the course of time, resort thither for employment, and become permanent settlers. Tea, it is believed, may be grown in sufficient quantity to supply the English market, and afford a handsome remuneration to the speculators. An inconsiderate expenditure of capital placed the Assam Tea Company in great jeopardy, and at one time it was feared the scheme would be abandoned. The number of managers and assistants appointed by the Assam Company to carry on their affairs, and superintend their tea gardens on large salaries, was quite unnecessary: one or two experienced European superintendents to direct the native establishment would have answered every purpose. A vast number of Coolies (or labourers) were induced to proceed to Upper Assam, on high wages, to cultivate the gardens; but bad arrangements having been made to supply them with proper wholesome food, many were seized with sickness. On their arrival at the tea-plantations, in the midst of high and dense tree jungle, numbers absconded, and others met an untimely end. The rice served out to the Coolies from the Assam Tea Company's store rooms, was so bad as not to be fit to be given to elephants, much less to human beings. The loss of these labourers, who had been conveyed to Upper Assam at a great expense, deprived the company of the means of cultivating so great an extent of country as would otherwise have been ensured; for the scanty population of Upper Assam offered no means of replacing the deficiency of hands. Another importation of labourers seems desirable, to facilitate and accomplish an undertaking formed under most auspicious circumstances. Nor was the improvidence of the Company in respect to labourers the only instance of their mismanagement. Although the Company must have known that they had no real use or necessity for a steamer, a huge vessel was nevertheless purchased, and frequently sent up and down the Burrampooter river from Calcutta; carrying little else than a few thousand rupees for the payment of their establishment in Upper Assam, which might have been transmitted through native bankers, and have saved the Company a most lavish and unprofitable expenditure of capital.

It is generally understood that too little attention had been paid to the advice of Major Jenkins, the Governor-General's Agent; or more vigilant supervision, better economy, and greater success might not unreasonably have been expected. The *cultivation* of tea in Assam, with a view of supplying the English market, was, it must be admitted, first contemplated by Major Jenkins; and for his exertions in having been the main cause of the Assam plant being proved to be the genuine tea of China, the Agricultural Society of Calcutta presented him with a gold medal; but the Assam tea was first *discovered* by Mr. Bruce in 1826, A.D

The tea of Assam is now becoming better known in the English market, and its quality more generally appreciated; and as the chief difficulties have been surmounted, every well-wisher of England and India must hope the directors will, in future, pursue a more scrutinizing and economical course: extending the cultivation of tea, and thereby, while enhancing the profits derivable from the concern, contribute to render England independent of China as far as tea is concerned. If Assam tea can be grown equal to the produce of China, there is little doubt but that, at the rate of one and sixpence the pound, a remunerating profit will accrue to the Company: a handsome, but not a too ample compensation for an enterprise involving such highly important considerations.

BOR ABORS, ABORS[4] AND MEREES.

THE BOR ABORS, ABORS, AND MEREES: their localities and origin—Ornaments of the women—Martial spirit of the Abors—Destitute of beards—Ignorant of reading or writing—Void of delicacy and cleanliness in their habits—Little known of the Abor country—Failure of Lieutenant Wilcox to ascend the Dehong river

The first of these three classes reside on the loftiest and most remote mountains north of the valley of Assam. The second class on a lower range, and the third at the foot of, or on the plains immediately leading up to, the hills. Several parties of Abors visited me frequently at Saikwah to barter a few fowls, eggs, ginger, chillies, yams, &c., for salt, and other necessaries of life. They appear to be descendants of the Tartar race; and are large, uncouth, athletic, fierce-looking, dirty fellows. The hair of the women is cut short, like that of the men: in a circle round the crown of the head it is two inches long, but the hair in front and behind, below the upper circle, is only about half an inch long. The ears of the men and women are perforated, the aperture, one inch in diameter, being distended by a piece of wood, worn as an ornament; and the necks of the Abor women are loaded with innumerable glass bead necklaces of all colours. Their arms are likewise adorned, from the wrist to the elbow with brass rings; the legs are exposed from the knee downwards, the calf of the leg being bandaged with cane rings to the ankle. The Abors are feared and respected by all the neighbouring tribes for their martial spirit; nevertheless they are in great dread of the highland or Bor Abors, who are said to be as brave as they are savage. Like all the hill tribes of Assam, the Abors are void of beards: invariably plucking them, and leaving only scanty moustaches. They can neither read nor write, and their language sounds extremely harsh. The dress of the Abor chiefs consists of Thibetian woollen cloaks, and a simple piece of cotton cloth, about a foot square, which is passed between the legs and suspended by a string round the waist: but not so effectually as to screen their persons from exposure every time they sit down. Of delicacy, however, the Abors are as void as they are of cleanliness. They wear three kinds of helmets, one of plain cane, and others trimmed with an edging of bear's skin, or covered with a thick yellow skin of a species of deer. A more formidable looking covering for the head could scarcely be worn.

---

[4] Abor is derived from the Assamese word *boree,* friendly; *aboree,* unfriendly. Thus we understand the term Abor Nagas, Abor Dufflahs, independent or hostile tribes; and this designation seems common to all rude tribes in Assam.

Abor cane helmets.

In December, 1835, an Abor chief, with two hundred followers, descended from the hills, and begged permission to locate on the Dehing, within a day's journey of Suddeah. The Political Agent asked the chief whether he was aware that the land in that quarter was within the Company's jurisdiction, and that settlers necessarily became subject to our police administration? He replied he was aware of that, and would readily give up any of his people guilty of criminal offences, but demurred to the introduction of our police officers for the apprehension of offenders. He was then asked whether he and his people would agree to pay taxes? His answer was that they had never been accustomed to do so, and could not submit to it.

From various reports, the Abors are deemed a very rude, barbarous people, but of open manners and warlike habits; their bluntness of expression is more manly and pleasing than the base servility and sycophancy of the Assamese. As they have been accustomed to levy contributions from the inhabitants of Seesee, and other districts in Assam, they would be dangerous neighbours, if located in the immediate vicinity of the Suddeah people.

Not acceding to the terms on which we were disposed to acquiesce in their application, the Abors returned to their hills. Scarcity of the means of subsistence was, it is supposed, the cause of their visit; and they evidently meditated replacing the Merees, who formerly laboured for the Abors on the Dehong quarter, but have since emigrated to Upper and Lower Assam, to escape the exactions of that tribe.

It appears that the Abors are not allowed to emigrate to Assam; for in 1844 two young men having eloped with two damsels to Saikwah, and the latter claiming protection from the British authorities, an inquiry was made as to the cause of their deserting their own country; when one freely confessed that her father had given her in marriage to an old man, but preferring a young Abor, she had determined on living with him in the Company's territory and disobeying her father's commands. The other stated that she had been given in marriage to a young man, who died, and she was retained for his younger brother, a mere boy; but not being disposed to wait until he had reached the age of puberty, she had fallen in love with an Abor youth, and trusted they might be permitted to pass their days in peace in the forests adjoining Saikwah. If their prayer was not granted, the girls affirmed, in the most earnest manner, that they should be tortured and sold to another tribe; while their young husbands would be cast into the Dehong river with their hands bound, to suffer death by drowning.

To the present day, little is known of the Abor country, Europeans never having been permitted to penetrate any very great distance into the interior. The eminent astronomer and adventurous traveller, Lieutenant Wilcox, in 1827, endeavoured to ascend the Dehong river, with the view of proving that this stream was the celebrated Sampoo river; but after a few days' journey he met with insuperable difficulties, from the rapidity of the current, the closeness of the country, and the absolute prohibition of the Abors against his proceeding farther. Since that period, no strenuous endeavours have been made to acquire further information regarding these rude barbarians. The Merees speak the Abor language, and a friendly intercourse exists between the tribes; though the Merees have ceased to bear the yoke of slavery or be subordinate to the Abors. Their chief occupation is husbandry, and they are generally considered a quiet and tolerably industrious race.

MISHMEES.

The Mishmees: divided into distinct clans—Their characteristics—Attire and ornaments of the women—Mishmees unrestricted in the number of wives—Inordinately fond of smoking—Very superstitious—Mode of settling disputes—Cane bridges—Feud between the Tain and Mezhoo Mishmees—Trade between the Lamas and Mishmees—Articles of barter and of produce—Names and number of followers of the chiefs

The Mishmee tribe reside in the hills on the north-east extremity of the valley of Assam. They are divided into several distinct clans. The Dibong Mishmees are called Chool Kutta or Crop-haired, and the others are known by the appellation of Tains and Mezhoos. They are a very wild, roaming race of people, constantly engaged in petty wars amongst themselves and their neighbours, the Abors and Singphoos, when the most remorseless reprisals and massacres are committed. They have no written language, and appear to belong to the Tartar race. They are of diminutive stature, but stout, active, and hardy; very dirty in their persons, and little encumbered with clothing. The chiefs wear the coarse red coloured woollens of Thibet, and the dress of the lower orders is extremely scanty. The women, however, are more decently attired; wearing a striped or coloured petticoat, or cloth folded round the waist, extending to the knees, and a kind of jacket or bodice, with a profusion of necklaces of several pounds weight, composed of porcelain, glass, and pieces of cornelian. The hair is bound up in a knot on the crown of the head, with a thin band of silver passing round the forehead. The lobe of the ears is hideously distended to an inch in diameter, to admit of the silver ear-ring being inserted: this mutilation of the ear evidently having been gradually effected from early youth. The Mishmees are not restricted in their number of wives; each man taking as many as he can afford to support. A curious custom is said to prevail as a preventive to the constant bickerings and jealousies natural to this system; each wife either has a separate house or store room, or she lives with her relations.

The Mishmees, women and children, as well as men, are inordinately fond of smoking; and use a roughly-made Singphoo bamboo pipe, or a brass China-made bowl, with a bamboo tube. A bag made of monkey's skin is suspended from a belt for the express purpose of carrying the tobacco pipe, flint and steel, with a leather case containing tinder. The men wear a long, straight sword, of China manufacture, ornamented with a tuft of coloured hair; and a lance, manufactured by themselves, is constantly carried. They also use the cross-bow and poisoned arrows. Their head dresses are composed of dog skin, fastened under the chin by strings.

Like all savages, they are superstitious; invoking an unknown spirit supposed to reside in the inaccessible mountains or dense forests; and on being afflicted by famine, sickness, or other misfortunes, they invariably sacrifice fowls and pigs, that the evil may be removed, and the wrath of the invisible spirit appeased by their offerings and submission. We are led to believe that the authority of the chiefs, though respected, is not absolute: they are obliged to abide by the decisions of the people, duly assembled for the purpose of settling disputes and arranging the amount of amercements to be imposed for offences committed. For all heinous crimes remission is said to be procurable by the liquidation of a fine; but adultery, if the husband be not privy to the offence, is punished by death, which is inflicted by the people purposely assembled for the trial.

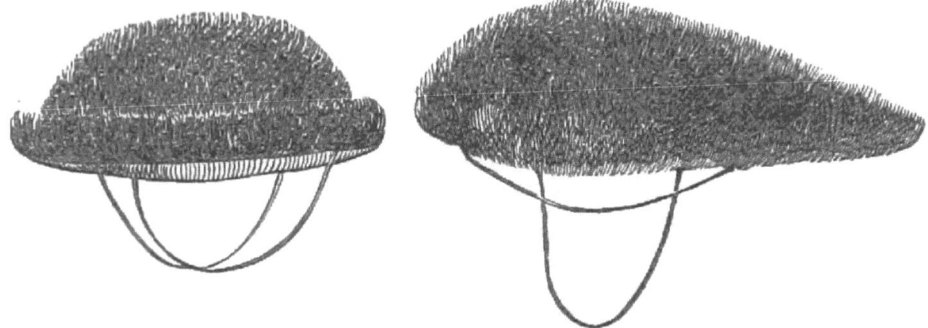

Mishmee Dog-skin caps.

The Mishmees, like the Abors, are most skilful in the construction of cane bridges; which they throw across rivers of eighty yards breadth. Three large cane ropes are sufficient to pass a person over in safety; but the transit, to any but a Mishmee, would be impracticable: for few would hazard the risk of falling into a rapid river below, or of being suspended midway on these ropes, unable to retire or advance. Accidents, however, rarely occur, and the Mishmees cross over their rivers in this manner without difficulty or apprehension.

In the year 1836, it was said that the Mezhoo and Tain, or Digaroo Mishmees had a serious quarrel about a marriage: for though at enmity often times with each other, and speaking a different dialect, they have not been debarred from intermarrying. Blows having been exchanged, the Mezhoo chief Rooling determined on speedily overcoming his enemies by an overwhelming force, and for this purpose he invited the Lamas to come to his assistance; which they did, and entered the Mishmee country with a force of seventy men, armed with matchlocks. The Tain Mishmees were totally defeated by the Lamas and Mezhoo Mishmees, and lost about twenty men. After this success, the Lamas returned to their own country about September 1836, and from that day we have had no similar invasion of this portion of Assam in favour of the Mezhoo Mishmees. No precise information is obtainable as to where these hostile operations occurred; but the conflict evidently took place several days' journey in advance of the villages visited by Lieutenant Wilcox in 1826–27, and by Dr. Griffiths in 1836–37. However, such was the heart-burning or feud between the Tains and the Mezhoos in 1836–37, that the late Dr. Griffiths, in his visit to the Mishmee country, could not by promises or bribes induce the Tains to furnish him with guides, even to the nearest village of the Mezhoos, or there can be little doubt that he would have succeeded in making good his way into the Lama country. In justification of their conduct, the Tains remarked, "If we give you guides, who is to protect us from the vengeance of the Mezhoos when you are gone? and who is to insure us from a second invasion of the Lamas?"

The Mishmee tribes were formerly obedient to the Assam Governors, the Suddeah Khawa Gohains: if they were not totally dependent, they at least gave small presents as tokens of submission, and attended to the orders of the Khamtees and Singphoos. In 1835, for example, the Duffa Gaum received considerable assistance from gangs of Mishmees sent down to erect his stockades. If under any pretence, therefore, the Thibetians, being a branch of the Chinese empire, should be permitted to establish their supremacy over the hill tribes in allegiance to the British Government in this quarter of the valley, our interests would be affected; but in the present rude state of society in this region there is little to be apprehended on this score. An immense, desolate, almost impassable tract, intervenes, so as to render ingress or egress from Assam to Thibet impracticable, excepting at certain seasons of the year. Traversing such a country, when the route follows the course of rivers, must naturally be difficult in the extreme. The hills are invariably characterized by excessive steepness, and as the greater portion of the route winds round them at some height above their bases, marching is excessively fatiguing, difficult, and dangerous. In many places a false step would be attended with fatal consequences: precipices must be crossed at a height of a hundred feet above the foaming bed of a river, the only support of the traveller being derived from the roots and stumps of trees and shrubs, and the angular character of the face of the rock. The paths are of the very worst description; always excessively narrow and overgrown by jungle in all directions. In very steep places the descent is often assisted by hanging canes, which afford good support, but no attempt is ever made to clear the paths of any obstruction: in fact, the natives seem to think the more difficult they are, the greater is their security against foreign invasions.

Notwithstanding these impediments to a free intercourse, some little trade, it is supposed, is carried on between the Mishmees and Lamas; the Mishmees exchanging their Bih (poison), Gathewan (an odoriferous root), Manjeet (madder), and Teetah (a bitter root, greatly esteemed for its medicinal qualities) for Lama cattle, brass pipes, gongs, and copper vessels; and if a friendly feeling of confidence could be established between the people of the plains of Assam and the Lamas, it is impossible to calculate to what extent the commerce between the two nations might attain. Once every year in the cold weather, that is between November and March, the Mishmees visit Suddeah for the purpose of bartering the only export produce of their country: namely, bih, teetah, manjeet, gathewan, gongs, brass pipes, and copper vessels; in exchange for which they invariably take, in preference to English merchandize, cows, buffaloes, and a quantity of small, coloured beads. Their cultivation is scanty: apparently not sufficient to supply their wants, and is, moreover, carried on in a very rude way. The ground selected as most favourable for cultivation lies on the slopes of hills, or on the more level patches occasionally bordering rivers. Some villages produce a good sort of hill rice, but their chief cultivation is ghoom dhan (or Indian corn), konee dhan, and two or three other inferior grains. The villages situated at low elevations produce excellent yams and aloos of several kinds. They are not acquainted with wheat, barley, &c., nor have they taken the trouble to grow potatoes, but that esculent is obtainable at Suddeah in great abundance. Of opium, a small quantity is cultivated, chiefly for sale to the Singphoos; though many of the natives are great opium-eaters. A small quantity of inferior cotton is also cultivated for the manufacture of their own clothing, and tobacco is in great request among them; they are likewise very fond of spirituous liquors.

We have no authentic data whereby to judge of the amount of the population, but from the following rough census of the followers of a few chiefs, it would not appear to be extensive.

No. of Chiefs.	Names of the different Chiefs.	No. of followers.
1	Jengsha	50
2	Japan	80
3	Deeling and Yeu	80
4	Galooms	80
5	Khoshas	100
6	Primsong	70
		460

The number of villages among which the above population is distributed, is seven; but there are two other villages, Muresas and Roolings, close to Khoshas. By far the greater number of villages appear to be located near the banks of the Lohit; one only has been observed on the Lung. The villages of Jengsha, Japan, Deeling, and Yeu, consist of several houses each; neither, however, exceeding ten in number. Ghalooms, Khoshas, and Primsong, consist each of a single house, capable of containing from eighty to one hundred and sixty persons. These comprehensive residences are divided by bamboo partitions into twenty or more rooms, all opening into a passage, in which the skulls of animals killed during the possessors' lifetime are duly arranged. The houses are all built on raised platforms, and the roofs are formed of the leaf of the arrow-root plant, or the leaves of cane, which are found in great abundance in all the forests. Khosha's house is one hundred and sixty feet in length; each room possessing a fire hearth; but as there are no chimneys, or any outlet for the smoke, excepting the door, a Mishmee dwelling is scarcely endurable.

Of Mishmee habits and customs little is known; feuds and misunderstandings having hitherto obstructed a freedom of intercourse indispensable to the acquirement of correct information. Several European officers have visited the Mishmee country for a few days, and have been desirous of proceeding by this route over the mountains north into the Lama country, or Thibet; to ascertain whether the celebrated Sampoo river flows into the Burrampooter from this quarter, or debouches into the Dehong, below Suddeah, or takes its course, as has been surmised, through China. This interesting inquiry, however, has not yet been solved; though little or no doubt appears to exist that the Sampoo joins the Burrampooter at one of these points. The British Government have hitherto, from prudential motives, abstained from giving offence to or exciting the jealousy of the Chinese, by permitting any of our officers to attempt to enter Thibet from the extreme north-eastern quarter of the valley of Assam. This is a sacrifice of geographical knowledge to policy; for there can be no question that a scientific traveller would obtain much information respecting the character of the country, and bring us acquainted with a people at present unknown to the civilized world.

DOOANEAHS.

The Dooaneahs: their origin—Nature of the country—Expert pioneers, but not of martial spirit—Strongly addicted to the use of opium

The Dooaneahs are descendants of Burmese or Singphoo fathers, from Assamese women, captured in predatory irruptions and kept as slaves. Assamese males, also carried off into slavery, are, from the loss of caste by their connection with the Singphoos, and the adoption of Singphoo habits, denominated Dooaneahs. They are a very hardy race, and inhabit the densest jungles; cultivating scarcely sufficient rice and opium for their maintenance, and subsisting, when their stock of grain is expended, on yams, kutchoos, and other roots of the forests. Without the aid of the Dooaneahs, no military detachment could move to many parts of the frontier, for none are so expert as pioneers. With the Dhao, or Singphoo short sword, they will cut a footpath through the densest jungles in the most expeditious manner, thus enabling our troops to move almost in any direction. They are not endowed with a martial spirit, and it is said they will not stand the fire of musketry; but if properly trained and disciplined, their fears might be surmounted. Their addiction, however, to opium is so great, that no permanent reliance could ever be placed in them as soldiers, in any emergency; and being utterly despised by their former masters, the Singphoos (from whose thraldom they have only lately escaped) it would seem inexpedient to place them in situations of trust, where the possibility of betrayal or defeat could be anticipated. The loss of their services as slaves, in cultivating the land, is deeply felt by the Singphoos; but these latter have not yet known the full extent of their inconvenience. In course of time few Dooaneah slaves will remain attached to the Singphoos; who must consequently either resort to manual labour themselves, or starve, or leave the province: which, by the way, would be the greatest boon we could desire, for the safety and improvement of our peaceable subjects.

ASSAMESE.

The Assamese: conquered and subjected to vassalage by the Ahooms—Mode of goverment—System of collecting the revenue—Conquered by the British in 1825—New system of taxation introduced—Abundance of gold—Gold washing—Natural products—Diet, clothing, &c.—Dwellings—Marriage—Betrothment—Marriage feast and presents—Breach of promise—Servitude for wives—Divorce—Slavery—Distribution of salt—Slavery—Ahoom dynasty—List of the last kings of Assam—Cruel punishments

The province of Assam was invaded about 1224 A.D., by a band of Ahoom or Shan adventurers; who conquered the country, parcelled out its territory, and subjected the population to a vassalage approximating to that in force under the feudal system of Europe. By this arrangement the whole body of cultivators were divided into different portions, called Khels, varying from one thousand to five thousand cultivators each. They were governed by officers of various grades: those called Borahs, possessing authority over twenty ghoots or sixty paicks; Sykeahs, over one hundred ghoots or three hundred paicks; and Huzarees, over one thousand; with one superior officer denominated a Kheldar, who was generally a nobleman, or person connected with the royal family. But in recent times this arrangement has been modified, and Borahs, Sykeahs, and Hazarees have exercised authority over a much smaller number of persons. The Kheldars collected the revenue and exercised jurisdiction in petty criminal offences. Owing to the backward state of society in Assam, and its almost utter destitution of commerce and manufactures, the revenue was seldom paid in money, but mostly in personal labour: all public buildings, roads, bridges, &c., were constructed out of the funds of labour at the command of the Government; and the services of all public functionaries, clerical, medical, military, and judicial, were paid in the same manner. To facilitate this arrangement, the community were divided into threes, (or in some parts of Assam fours) each division being called a ghote; and if one of the three served the state throughout the year, the other two were excused the payment of money, revenue, or produce. From artizans and manufacturers, who were subjected to a higher taxation than other classes, money was taken occasionally; but more frequently the tax was levied in produce.

Under the Ahoom Government the monopoly of office was at first confined to the Ahooms, or original conquerors of the soil; but in the reign of Rodroo Sing, 1695, A.D., when the Assamese natives of the soil had become proselytes to the

Hindoo religion, they were admitted to a share in the public employ. When the British Government conquered the country in 1825, this system of revenue, founded upon personal labour, was still in existence; but a money rate of taxation under the form of a poll-tax was introduced as far as circumstances would allow, the rates being fixed with reference to the customs of the ancient government. The two poorahs of land allowed to each cultivator were deemed equivalent to two English acres: the land could not be taken from him as long as he paid his revenue, but it was nevertheless considered the property of the state and could not be disposed of by the tenant. Almost the whole of the land in Assam is now taxed according to its quality, at so much per poorah or acre, but in some places any quantity of land may be cultivated by paying a certain sum per plough. The poll tax is likewise collected where the population is unsettled and scanty.

The religious wants of the people were provided for by the Assam rulers apportioning a certain number of paicks or cultivators to each Shuster or temple, for the support of which one-half of their revenue was assigned: the other half was appropriated by Government. Independently of this, grants of land were made to various religious persons, under the title of Debootur (service of the Gods), Dhurmooter (religious purposes), and Bramooter, for the support of the Brahmins (or priests); and a remission of half the usual rate of taxation was allowed when the claims of the parties were fairly established.

Assam is noted for the abundance of gold found in many of its rivers; and as the manner of acquiring it by washing the sands may not be generally known, and is a subject of considerable importance, a description may not be uninteresting to the reader. In the first place, the gold washer, taught by experience, chooses a favourable site; a wooden trough, six feet long by one and a half broad and two inches and a half deep, is then placed on pegs driven into the sand: one end of the trough being raised to throw it into an inclined or sloping position. This effected, a shifting bamboo sieve, made to fit the trough, is placed upon it; two men with baskets then strew a plentiful coat of sand and gravel from the river on the sieve, through which the gold washer quickly washes the sand by pouring water on it, and shaking the sieve to hasten the descent of the water into the trough. By this means the heavier particles sink and the lighter are carried off by the stream, that continues to flow from the square or upper end of the trough to the circular end, from which it escapes by an aperture purposely bored. The coarse gravel on the sieve is frequently removed, and a fresh supply is continually heaped up, until the sand in the bottom of the trough containing the gold is about an inch thick. The sieve is then removed, and placed at one end of the trough, and a quantity of water being poured through the sieve, it falls on the sand like a shower of rain, till all the light particles are carried off by the stream flowing down the trough. By this process the heavier particles only remain, and these are gold dust and iron. The gold dust being now distinctly visible, is subjected to a further washing, and then dexterously floated on to leaves; after which it is transferred to a glazed earthen vessel, and again washed with the hand. The gold washer now daubs his hands with lime, and having applied some quicksilver and water, again washes the sand with his hands, which causes a scum to rise on the surface; this being cleared off, after repeated washings, the gold is found adhering to the quicksilver, when it is taken from shell to shell till every particle of sand is removed. The quicksilver and gold dust are then placed in a shell on a charcoal fire, and with the aid of a bamboo blow-pipe the ore is speedily melted; a little water being then applied, the gold is separated and forms a ball at the bottom of the shell. It is considered a good return if three persons at one trough can obtain four annas weight of gold (worth three rupees) in twelve days: giving the labourer one anna four pice per diem. At one time there was a numerous body of gold washers employed in collecting gold from many of the rivers in Upper and Central Assam; and the rivers were, in some instances, let by Government to persons wishing to enjoy the sole monopoly of bringing gold into the market. The profit on the gold dust must have been very considerable, seeing that it realized from twelve to fifteen rupees per tolah, and was produced in large quantities. But, like many other monopolies, this was found open to abuse: the people were oppressed for the benefit of the manufacturers, and the Government deemed it expedient to discontinue it as a source of revenue; thus leaving one of the most valuable products of the province neglected. Gold, in consequence, is becoming scarce; and we hope, therefore, that the evil will work its own cure, by stimulating the gold washers to resume their ancient lucrative vocation.

In many parts of the province, coal of a good quality, is found; and indeed the soil of Assam generally may be considered extremely rich: it abounds in valuable products, such as rice, sugar-cane, moongah silk, pepper, mustard-seed, and cotton. But the bounty of nature is marred by the indolence and apathy of man: the cultivator seldom looks beyond his immediate wants, and makes no attempt to improve his condition. In fact, in agricultural, commercial, and manufacturing industry, this country may be considered at least a century behind Bengal; and there seems little prospect of improvement, excepting by the introduction of a more active and industrious people, who might stimulate the natives to increased exertions. An inveterate indulgence in the use of opium by the population at large, is the curse of the country: depressing the industry and withering the physical energies of the people, by limiting their desires to the gratification of the wants of the day.

The greater portion of the Assamese are Hindoos; but they are very lax in their observance of the rites of the Hindoo religion, and in the few ceremonies which they do perform, deviate considerably from the strict tenets enjoined by that creed. In their domestic habits they are simple in the extreme; their poverty and ignorance limiting their desires within the narrowest compass. A slight cotton covering thrown over the shoulders, and a dhoti or sheet tied round the waist, reaching to the knees, forms the chief clothing of the poor: shoes are never worn. A little oil, rice, vegetables (such as greens and chillies), seasoned with the smallest quantity of salt, and sometimes a few small fish, compose the humble fare of the poor peasant. These necessaries are procurable for about three shillings per mensem, and as the wages of a day labourer or coolie are from one and a half to two annas per diem, or about two rupees per mensem, he has still one shilling to spare..

An Assamese gentleman, and a Meree woman.

This spare diet has, of course, its influence upon the stature and bulk of the Assamese; who are, consequently, slender, effeminate, and indolent. Their complexion is not uniform; numbers being very fair, and as many excessively dark. Their morals are exceedingly depraved, and their manners servile and contemptible. Nor are the women one whit superior to the men; and although they are far from possessing attractive persons, they are utter slaves to the worst licentiousness.

The dwellings of the Assamese are of the meanest description imaginable: there are no stone or brick houses[5] in the country; a simple hut, ten feet by twenty, divided into a couple of rooms for sleeping and sitting in, or not uncommonly one solitary room, form the only accommodation a man, wife, and family possess. The hut is about ten feet high, with a grass roof, and the walls are made of reeds plastered outside, and sometimes inside also, with mud and cow-dung. A small platform of bamboos, two feet high, serves as a bedstead; and a seetulpattee, or grass mat, constitutes the amount of bedding, without any other covering than the clothes that are worn during the day. Many Assamese, however, prefer the bare ground, with a simple mat as a bed. The earth floor is daily plastered with mud and cow-dung: the cow being held sacred amongst the Hindoos, its ordure has, it is considered, the peculiar property of not only cleansing, but purifying their habitations. Its use certainly gives their huts a tidy appearance, and worms and insects are not so troublesome as they would otherwise be.

These frail buildings require yearly repairs, but the peasants are put to no expense for them, except in bringing posts, reeds, and grass from the jungle. Assamese families of respectability and wealth live in larger houses of the same character of architecture; but instead of one hut, they erect several close together, in the form of a square, each hut opening into the quadrangular court-yard, which is entered by a portico or receiving room for visitors.

In the estimation of the Assamese, marriage is one of the most important duties of life; not only for the additional comfort, assistance, and respectability it confers on the man, but because he considers he has not fulfilled the divine will if he has failed to take unto himself a wife—and sometimes a plurality of wives. Polygamy is prevalent throughout the province, and is only limited in extent by the means of each man to provide for the support of his wives. If a man marries only one or two wives, he probably has on his establishment three or four concubines; and his life is therefore embittered and harassed by perpetual family quarrels. It is the custom in Assam for parents to make early arrangements for the marriage of their sons; and having selected the daughter of any particular family of the same caste, a regular agreement is entered into for the amount of the dower to be paid to the parents of the girl, even when she is but a mere child. The first ceremony of betrothing the girl is called Tamul pankatta, or partaking of the betel nut and leaf of the betel vine; which takes place when the damsel may be about four years of age. The parents of the youth proceed to the house of the family with whom they wish to form a matrimonial alliance, make their proposal, and produce a present

[5] In many parts of Assam there are many fine temples and old forts built of stone and bricks; but, the art of making such firm and durable bricks as were used in former days seems now to be entirely lost.

of the following articles:—

	Rs.	Ans.	Pice.
Betel nut and betel leaf	1	0	0
Two bhars (or baskets) of milk	0	8	0
Fish	0	4	0
Treacle	0	4	0
Plantains	0	4	0
Chura (parched rice)	0	4	0
Total rupees	2	8	0

If the above present be accepted, then, to all intents and purposes, the agreement is ratified between the parties, and is considered as solemnly and legally binding as are the parchment instruments which regulate these contracts in England. The next ceremony performed in furtherance of the union of the young people is called Nowae toolun (or attaining the period of puberty), when the girl being about ten or eleven years of age, the youth's parents proceed to her house again with another present composed of the following articles:—

	R.	Ans.	Pice.
Oil	1	0	0
Red vermilion, for the distinguishing mark of the tutelary deity on the forehead	0	2	0
Betel nut and betel leaf	0	4	0
Pitter goorie (rice flour)	0	4	0
Akho rice parched in the husk, (dhan)	0	4	0
Total rupees	1	14	0

About six months or a year after this offering, the third ceremony takes place, and is called "Kharoo munee puredheen" (or putting the bracelets and necklaces on the bride). The expense incurred on these occasions corresponds with the means of the bridegroom and his parents. To show the nature of the presents made, we subjoin the following list:—

	Rs.	Ans.	Pice.
Bracelets	20	0	0
Ear-rings	12	0	0
Necklaces of several strings, of various sizes and colours	5	0	0
Madulee, a silver charm ornament suspended from the neck	1	8	0
Four silver finger-rings, 4 annas each	1	0	0
One piece of Mongah silk cloth, five cubits long	1	8	0
Betel nut and betel leaf	2	0	0

Twelve bhars (or baskets) of treacle, rice, curds, pittagoorie kutcha (ground rice) chandagoorie puckah (baked rice flour): each basket valued at four annas each	3	0	0
Total rupees	46	0	0

The fourth and last ceremony is Shadee (or marriage), when a great feast is given at the damsel's house by her parents to the friends of both families. The presents consist of:—

	Rs.	*Ans.*	*Pice.*
Fish, rice, diel, oil, salt, greens, and chillies	3	0	0
Betel nut and betel leaf	1	0	0
One piece of Moongah silk	1	8	0
One Burkopper cotton cloth, for the girl's father or brother	1	0	0
Gao dhun, dower or price of the girl, paid to her parents in ready cash	9	0	0
Total rupees	15	8	0

The bridegroom is kept awake all night by feasting, dancing, and singing; and in the morning, all having broken their fast, the bridegroom accompanies his bride to his own dwelling in a regular procession. Drums, cymbals, and gongs take the lead; the bride follows either in a palkee, or mounted on a pony; or, if very poor, she walks in the midst of her female acquaintances, covered from head to foot with a white cotton cloth or veil thrown loosely over her; and the bridegroom and his friends bring up the rear. On arrival at the bridegroom's house, his friends partake of a repast, and return to their homes in the course of the afternoon. The young couple then take up their abode, generally in a newly erected house adjoining their parents' dwelling. The whole expense of the marriage conducted on this scale amounts to sixty-five rupees fourteen annas; but only the better orders disburse such a sum. If the parties are in very affluent circumstances, however, many hundreds of rupees are expended. The poorer class, from inability to incur further outlay, are not unfrequently married at the second ceremony of Nowae toolun for four or five rupees, including every expense.

Should the parents of the girl, contrary to the marriage contract or betrothment, give their daughter to another person, it is incumbent on them to refund the value of the presents they may have received on different occasions for a number of years previously. Yet in few countries, probably, will the number of violated contracts or promises of marriages be found to exceed those of Assam. The litigation and ill-will consequent on these ill-advised agreements is incalculable, and the complaints under this head in the civil courts are innumerable.

There is a remarkable similarity between one of the customs in Assam and that practised by the Patriarchs of old. Jacob served Laban as a servant or bondsman many years to obtain in marriage Leah and Rachel, who were sisters; and he was not allowed to marry the younger before the elder. So in Assam a man may marry two sisters, but he must marry the elder before the younger. It is not uncommon, when a man is poverty stricken, to engage to live and work for several years for the father of the girl he wishes to marry. He is then called a Chapunea, a kind of bondsman, and is entitled to receive bhat kupper, food and clothing, but no wages; and at the expiration of the period of servitude, if the girl does not dislike him, the marriage takes place. The man is looked on in the family as a khanu damad (or son-in-law), and is treated kindly. If the girl's father be very wealthy, and he has no sons, he will sometimes select, from some equally respectable family, a husband for his daughter, and bring him up in his own house. The youth so selected is likewise called a Chapunea, and inherits the whole of his father-in-law's property. If a woman's husband dies, though she may be only eighteen or twenty years of age, she can never marry again. She is considered a Baree, or widow for life; but very few women—if any—so circumstanced lead a life of celibacy: they prefer submitting to be selected as companions, and are then contemptuously designated batuloo (refuse or offal). And this condition of existence among the lower orders is almost as common as marriage; for the becoming a man's Dhemuna stree (alias mistress or companion) involves no expense for bhar bhete (marriage present) or gaodhun (dower), and is therefore more convenient. The offspring of this connection inherit all the rights of legitimate issue, and are not the less respected in society; there is, therefore, no bar to the loose and immoral habits so prevalent among the poorer classes in Assam. The indulgence of these is further facilitated by the ease with which the marriage-tie may be dissevered. No reference is necessary to either the temporal or ecclesiastical courts: dissolution is simply effected by the husband, if displeased with his wife or doubtful of her fidelity. On these occasions he merely assembles his friends, and in their presence addresses his wife in these words:—"Henceforth I look on you as my mother and sister;" and tearing a betel leaf into two pieces the marriage is dissolved, and the man and woman are free to select fresh partners. The divorce is equally complete if the husband distributes a little salt to each member of the assembly of friends, making the same speech to the wife. The Cacharies, a simple-minded, honest, and industrious tribe of Assamese, cut off a branch of the kuddum tree before a select body of friends, when the husband declares he has divorced his wife, and the ceremony is completed.

The funeral obsequies of the Assamese are performed agreeably to Hindoo usages. The body is burnt as soon as possible after death. Jogees, Weavers, and Cacharies bury their dead in the same manner as Moossulmans. A curious practice prevails amongst the Assamese of giving salt to their friends assembled to bear witness to many of the common occurrences of life. If a man adopts a son, he distributes salt to his friends in token of a person having been appointed to succeed to his property. If he buys a piece of land or purchases a slave, or if a dispute is settled by arbitrators, salt is in like manner distributed amongst a few friends who testify to the fairness of the transaction; and amongst themselves these agreements or settlements are as binding as laws could make them.

When an Assamese has been excommunicated by the priests for any civil offence, the expiation of his crime and his restoration to society are effected by the payment of a fine, called chundrayen, amounting to four rupees: dhurmdund (twelve annas), feeding the Punchayet or jury, (one rupee) at most about six rupees. If the offender be very poor, one rupee ten annas will suffice to pay for "purachit" (absolution); which is granted by the priest.

By the ancient Assam laws, slavery existed in a variety of forms. All born of a free slave by a free father, as well as those of pure slave parentage, were considered slaves. Free women married to slaves became, with their offspring, slaves. The king had the power to grant to his nobles and spiritual advisers portions of the free population as slaves, which the owner could dispose of in any manner he thought proper: they were designated Bohoteahs. Prisoners of war were often granted to individuals as slaves; and criminals who had a sentence of death passed upon them had it commuted to slavery, and were assigned to certain masters. The free people were at liberty to mortgage themselves for debts; remaining in bondage for a number of years or until the sum borrowed was paid off; and as the debtor was seldom in a situation to liquidate his obligation, he continued a slave to his creditor for the remainder of his life. In each district the value of slaves varied considerably.

Name of District.	Value of Men.	Value of Boys.			Value of Women.	Value of Girls.		
	Rs.	*Rs.*		*Rs.*	*Rs.*	*Rs.*		*Rs.*
Kamroop	40	15	to	20	20	12	to	20
Durrung	20	10	to	15	15	8	to	12
Nowgong	20	10	to	15	15	8	to	12

The above is the estimated value of good castes, such as Kuletahs, Kewuts, Kooches. The price of the lower castes, denominated Joges, Doomes, Cachares, Boreahs, and Burahees, was one-third less.

In the present brief review of Assam it would be foreign to our object to attempt to describe the events of each reign; we confine ourselves, therefore, to a short list of the last kings of Assam. (See opposite page.)

The downfall of the Ahoom kings of Assam may be attributed to their becoming proselytes to the Hindoo religion in the reign of Jeydhoj Singh, A.D. 1654; to the religious persecutions of the Muttucks in the reign of Seeb Singh; to family dissensions and disputes, and the cruel treatment of Mohun Burjona Gohain. Rodur Singh left five sons, Seb Singh, Prumutta Singh, Mohun Burjona Gohain, Rajeswur Singh, and Luckme Singh. The third son, Mohun Burjona Gohain, being marked with the small-pox, was incapacitated to reign; and his younger brother, Rajeswur Singh, superseded him. By the evil machinations of the Bor Borowa, Rajeswur Singh was led to believe his brother, Mohun Burjona Gohain, was plotting against his government; and for the effectual suppression of this conspiracy, his brother was expelled the capital in the most ignominious manner, his ears having been slit and one of his eyes plucked out.

List of the Last Kings of Assam.

1681, A.D., Gudhadhur Singh.

1695, A.D., Bodur Singh.

1714, A.D., Seeb Singh.

1744, A.D., Prumutta Singh.

1751, A.D., Rajeswur Singh.

1769, A.D., Luckme Singh.

1780, A.D., Gowree Nath Singh.

1795, A.D., Kumuleswur Singh.

1810, A.D., Chunderkant Singh.

1817, A.D., Poorunder Singh.

1818, A.D., Chunderkant Singh reinstated on the throne by the Burmese.

1821, A.D., Jogessur Singh placed on the throne by the Burmese.

1824–25, A.D., Assam conquered by the British troops, and the Burmese army expelled the province.

1833, A.D., Poorunder Singh made Rajah of Upper Assam, April 12th, 1833, and deposed by the British Government, Aug. 1835, A.D.

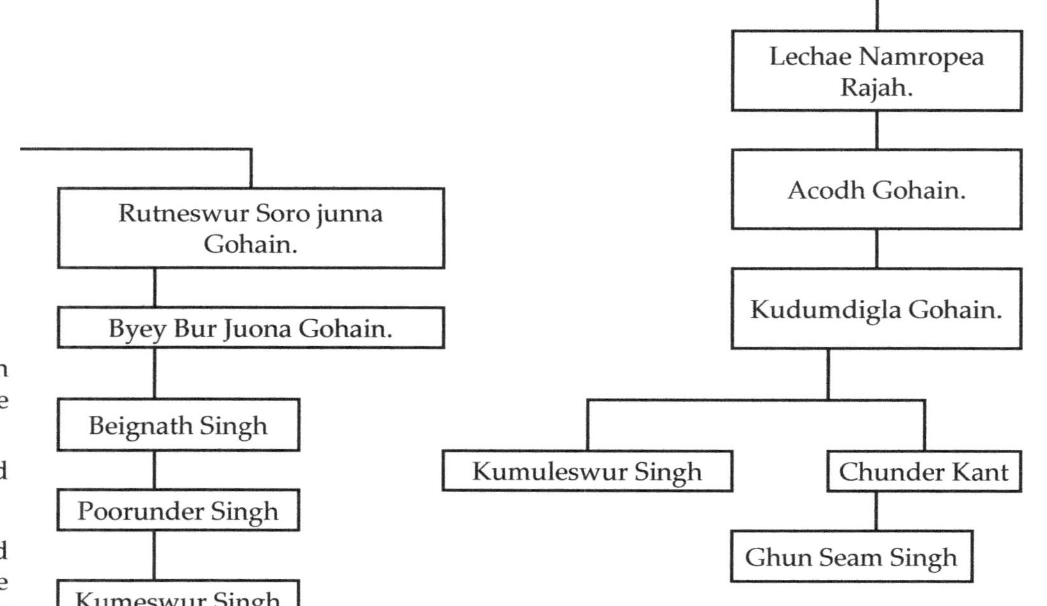

It was, doubtless, as we have already remarked, from this severity that the prince Mohun Burjona Gohain, in the succeeding reign of his younger brother, Luckme Singh, was induced to rebel against his sovereign, and to join the Muttucks, hoping thereby to avenge his wrongs and gain the throne; but though temporary success attended the Muttuck insurrection, the Prince failed in realizing his ambitious projects, and hastened the extinction of the power of the Ahoom dynasty.

In no part of the world, perhaps, have such sanguinary customs and laws prevailed as in Assam, under the Ahoom kings. Many of their punishments were revolting to humanity. Criminals were whipped, put in the pillory, impaled; their limbs amputated, the nose, ears, and lips mutilated; the hair was torn out by the roots, eyes were plucked out of the sockets, and sometimes offenders were ground between wooden rollers, sawn asunder, or tortured with red-hot irons. A variety of other cruelties were practised with a relentlessness that but too vividly marked the barbarity of the rulers of those days, and rendered it a matter of sincere congratulation that a merciful providence shortened the period of their sovereignty, and placed the country in the hands of the British Government, in 1824–25.

NAGAS.

THE NAGAS: their general features and characteristics—Missionary efforts by the American Baptists—Naga Government—Treatment of strangers—Omens—Husbandry—Salt wells—Mode of warfare—Ceremony of tattooing—Mode of revenge—Naga customs—Funeral ceremonies—List of the Naga tribe

The south-eastern hills of Assam are the abode of many tribes of Nagas. They are a very uncivilized race, with dark complexions, athletic sinewy frames, hideously wild and ugly visages: their faces and bodies being tattoed in a most frightful manner by pricking the juice of the bela nut into the skin in a variety of fantastic figures. They are reckless of human life; treacherously murdering their neighbours often without provocation, or at best for a trivial cause of offence. The greater number of the Nagas are supposed to be in a very destitute state, living almost without clothing of any kind. Their poverty renders them remarkably free from any prejudices in respect of diet: they will eat cows, dogs, cats, vermin, and even reptiles, and are very fond of intoxicating liquors.

Amongst a people so thoroughly primitive, and so independent of religious prepossessions, we might reasonably expect missionary zeal would be most successful; for the last eight years, however, two or three American Baptist missionaries have in vain endeavoured to awake in them a sense of the saving virtues of Christianity. For a considerable period the residence of the missionaries was at Suddeah; where their labours, I believe, were unattended by any conversions either of Assamese or Singphoos. On the station being deserted by the troops for Saikwah, in 1839, the missionaries turned their attention more particularly towards the Nagas; they took up their residence on the Boree Dehing river, at Jeypore, established a school, and were indefatigable in endeavouring to gain some correct knowledge of the savage tribes in their vicinity. A few years' experience here proved the futility of their plans. Instead of wandering amongst the savage tribes scattered over an immense extent of country, in unhealthy, dense jungles, it would have been prudent and politic to have afforded instruction in the first instance to the populous villages in the plains. One or more natives have been baptized at Jeypore, agreeably to the rites of the Baptist persuasion, by immersion in the Boree Dehing river, and this is the sum total of the missionary success. This has, it is understood, induced them to change their abode to Seebsauger and Nowgong, where they seem to think there is a greater chance of their succeeding. The missionaries have a printing press, and many elementary books of instruction in Assamese and English have been printed by them for the use of the natives.

Their exemplary conduct and exertions merit the utmost commendation, and it is to be deplored that their well-intentioned labours should not be crowned by felicitous results.

Nagas.

To this day little is known either of the country inhabited by the Nagas, or of their habits and customs. Several officers have penetrated a considerable distance into the hills occupied by the Nagas; but always with marked and necessary caution, attended by a military guard. Greater intercourse between the highland Nagas and the people of the plains were much to be wished; but it is doubtful if any advantage would accrue to the British Government from extending its sway southward, over immense tracts of unprofitable wastes or dense jungles thinly inhabited.

Naga Government.

Under the ancient Assam Government some of the tribes may have been more dependent upon the Government than they are now, but the Naga territory was never considered an integral portion of the sovereignty of Assam. It is customary with the Naga tribe to offer trifling presents to the British authorities, as a mark of submission, and something is given in return, in token of amicable feeling; but the Nagas have never been considered subject to our regular jurisdiction, and nothing in the shape of an assessment has ever been imposed upon them.

It is very difficult to arrive at anything like a correct understanding of the nature of the feuds between neighbouring tribes; for the Nagas have no written language, and their dialects vary considerably in different parts of the country. No general government exists over the whole tribe: they are divided into innumerable clans, independent of each other, and possessing no power beyond the limits of their respective territories. Each tribe seems ever jealous of its neighbour; and cruel hostilities, ending in the most tragical manner—even to the extermination of a tribe and the total destruction of its cattle, stores, and property—are often the result of their mutual animosity. The form of the Naga government is democratical; each clan seems to be ruled by a president and two subordinates or deputies, who form the executive. The president is called Khonbao, and the deputies Sundekae and Khonsae: the one prime minister, and the latter a chief over twenty houses. The chief magistrate or arbitrator, the Khonbao, decides all disputes of a civil or criminal nature, and it is optional with him either to direct or enforce his orders with his own sword; but in all this he is merely the organ or agent of the people, for the decisions are the results of the consultations of the whole Raj, or populace, who discuss all matters of importance in the open Moorung, or hall of justice, to be found in every Naga village. The Khonbao, Sundekae, and Khonsae, on these occasions, summon all the community to attend and assist with their counsel in disposing of any affairs of moment: such as a war to be undertaken against a foe, or in furtherance of revenge; or the punishment of crimes committed by any of the members of the tribe in opposition to their established polity.

The dignity of Khonbao is hereditary: the eldest son of the incumbent invariably succeeding to the title and authority. No junior brother can assume the rank, under any pretensions founded on greater ability, personal appearance, or reputation of valour. In the event of the Khonbao leaving no progeny, his wife succeeds to his title and authority; and the deputy Khonbao, Sundekae and Khonsae in council enforce her commands, and report everything to her connected with the welfare of the community.

No hospitality is shown to a stranger visiting the Naga country, unless he visits the Khonbao in the first instance: he is unable, even under the greatest distress, to obtain shelter or provision elsewhere. On the arrival of an embassy it is conducted to the residence of the Khonbao, who gives audience immediately, and returns a reply by the messengers on his own responsibility, if the object of the visit is of no great importance. But, on the other hand, should the embassy be for the purpose of obtaining redress of wrongs committed by the clan of the Khonbao, the embassy is retained and entertained hospitably till the Sundekae, Khonsae, and principal elders of the people can be assembled in the moorung; when the grievance is stated and inquiries made, each member stating openly and candidly his opinion on the matter at issue. The Khonbao propounds what is, in his opinion, expedient and best for the public good; but if there appears any irregularity, the people express their disapprobation to the Khonbao, and he is constrained to abide by the will of the community, to give orders to the embassy, and allow its departure to the place whence it came. In this manner all affairs and discussions are regulated amongst the Nagas. Any attempt to travel through their country, unaccompanied by a person acquainted with the roads, villages, and Naga language, would be the height of folly; as the traveller would not be supplied with water, food, or fire, neither would any shelter be afforded him, and his life would be in imminent danger.

Omens.

The superstition of the Nagas is strikingly exhibited in the great attention paid by them to all signs of good and evil, before they attempt the execution of any project: whether it be to prepare the land to receive the seed, to proceed on hunting or fishing excursions, or to enter upon any war expedition. On these occasions the Khonbao, Sundekae, and Khonsae, assemble the people, and a grand consultation is held between the chief ruler and the elders of the village, in order to divine the most auspicious moment, and to ascertain whether the affair under consideration will turn out favourably or otherwise. To aid the deliberation, new-laid eggs are procured, which they address in these terms:—"Oh eggs, you are enjoined to speak the truth and not to mislead us by false representations." The eggs are then perforated and roasted on a fire, and the yolk is minutely examined: if it appears entire, the omen is considered good; if broken, the reverse, and auspicious for their enemies. In this conclusion the senate are likewise confirmed by a peculiar appearance of the white of the egg. Another simple mode of divining the propriety or expediency of carrying out certain plans is by burning the Bujjal bamboo. Should it crackle and fall out of the fire on the left side, it is a good omen; should it fly out on the right, the event is accepted as a warning of failure and disaster. By these simple and strange proceedings are the acts of these people guided.

Husbandry.

In their agricultural operations, the implements of the Nagas are simple and rude in the extreme; but bullocks and buffaloes are used as in Assam. At the commencement of the season, the Khonbao having assembled the people after the usual ceremonies of consulting the omens, the land is apportioned out to each clan, the jungle is cleared, and sowing commences. Konee dhan, a small grain, and Indian corn, or goom dhan, is sown in January and gathered in about June, when the Behoo is celebrated with great festivities; resembling the old English custom of harvest-home. After the goom dhan and konee dhan is cut, ahoo dhan is sown; and after this crop, kuchoos, a kind of root resembling the arrow root, are planted; so that in the course of the year three crops are raised from the same land. This is done for three successive years; when, the land being impoverished, new land is broken up for the same period, until the usual time of fallow admits of the old land being again resumed. Yet, with all the means of avoiding famine, blessed with a fertile soil and a wonderful rapidity of vegetation, so improvident are these savages, that in a few months the whole produce of the land is consumed, and they are compelled to subsist on roots and leaves of the forests till the return of harvest.

Salt Wells.

In different parts of the Naga territory many salt wells exist, and being worked by some of the tribes an immense quantity of salt is produced. This is sold or bartered to the people of Assam for rice, and by this means, doubtless, the miseries attendant on a scanty supply of food are greatly lessened. We have no means of judging of the extent of the salt trade between the Assamese and Nagas, but the commerce might doubtless be increased by greater vigilance, to the mutual advantage of both parties.

Preparations for War.

When the Nagas purpose taking vengeance on a neighbouring tribe, the Khonbao assembles the elders of the village; and, in accordance with established customs, the omens being consulted and proving propitious, a plan to cut up their enemies by surprise is decided on. Each man provides himself with a spear, sword, bamboo choong, a hollow joint of the bamboo filled with water, and a small basket of rice; and, the party being formed, set out in the day towards the frontier of the enemy who is to be attacked. At night they cross over and occupy a favourable position in ambush, surrounding the enemy's village. There they take their repast, and when the cock first crows on the following morning, they rush, with great shouting, into the village, and cut up every body they meet with; sparing neither old infirm men, nor helpless women, nor children: even the cows, pigs, and poultry of the foe are slaughtered. Sometimes the victors remain on the spot two or three days, but generally return to their own village on the same day; taking with them the heads, hands, and feet of those they have massacred: these they parade about from house to house, accompanied with drums and gongs, throwing liquor and rice on the heads, and uttering all manner of incantations: saying, "Call your father, mother, and relations to come here and join you in eating rice and drinking spirits, when we will kill them with the same sword." They then sing, dance, and perform all manner of anticks; pierce and mangle the heads of their enemies, and again with curses enjoin them to summon their whole race to suffer the same ignominious treatment. In the massacre, one of the Nagas may have, perhaps, particularly distinguished himself by evincing great ferocity in cutting off more heads than any of his party; which circumstance he fails not to bring to the notice of his assembled friends. Stalking out before them he challenges them to mark his deeds, and with many songs of boisterous mirth and audacious boasting, he drags the heads of his enemies about in the most contemptuous manner, proclaiming his own triumph somewhat after this fashion:—

"In the world I am the most powerful and courageous; there is none equal to me. I am the greatest of all men. No one" (pointing to the skulls of his enemies) "can perform such deeds. Like to the clouds that thunder and hurl down fire-balls into the water to the destruction of the fish,—like to the tiger who leaps out to seize the deer,—like to the hawk who pounces down on the chickens and carries them off, do I cut up every one, and carry off their heads; and with these weapons" (dashing them together, to produce a clashing noise) "I have killed such and such persons: yes, I have killed them. You know my name. The greatest beast of the forest, the elephant, I first destroy, and after that all other animals too insignificant to mention. Such a hero am I, there is no one equal to me," &c. &c.

The same scene is enacted for three or four successive days; when the heads being hacked and sufficiently danced about to satiate Naga revenge, they are suspended from the branches of Nahor trees. After this, the ceremony of tattooing the body is performed, and a most severe operation it is. The burnt ashes of a pot are pricked into the skin with the thorns of the cane: a great quantity of blood exudes, and the body swells to a great size. Being previously thrown into a state of stupid intoxication, the patient is left to welter in the dirt and blood for three days, unconscious of his condition. After this operation, the young sprouts of the Bhat-teeta tree being well pounded, are smeared over the wounds, and in the course of twenty-five days the patient is able to resume his avocations; upon which a number of pigs and fowls are killed, and a great feast is given; the heads of the enemies being brought down from the trees and strewed out upon a platform before the populace in the court, or Raj Moorung. For a whole month from the day of the massacre, the Nagas daily sing the war song quoted above, and dance and manifest the greatest excitement and delight.

All villages are not entitled to the honour of retaining the heads of their enemies; they must be kept in the village of the Khonbao.

In some Naga villages it is the custom, for a man who has committed murder in cutting off the head of a foreigner, to be joined by ten or a dozen Nagas in submitting to the operation of tattooing; which in such cases is an indispensable ceremony. The tattooing is pricked round the calves of the legs in ten or twelve rings or circles interspersed with dots; the thighs, the breast, the neck, the fingers, the back of the hand, the arms, the forehead, and nose, the vicinity of the eyes and the ears being similarly decorated. The poorest Naga peasant deems it an honour to have his body thus embellished with stripes, figures, and dots; and the omission of the ceremony would entail on him eternal disgrace and censure. Indeed, the tattooing determines the character and consequence of the individual; for by certain marks on one arm it is apparent that he has killed a man; when both arms and body are scarred he is known to have murdered two individuals; and when the face and eye-sockets are indelibly impressed with the tattoo, he stands proclaimed the assassin of three of his fellow-creatures, and is thenceforth esteemed a valiant warrior.

Angamee Naga warrior.

On the question being once put to the Nagas whether they would like to become the subjects of the Company, they promptly replied,—"No: we could not then cut off the heads of men and attain renown as warriors, bearing the honourable marks of our valour on our bodies and faces."

If a Naga happens to be suddenly surprised, and cut off by the inhabitants of a neighbouring village, his corpse is quickly taken up by his friends and placed on a platform in the jungles near the road. At the expiration of three or four days they perform some ceremonies, and wait till a favourable opportunity occurs for avenging his death. The purpose is never relinquished, though its execution may unavoidably be tardy: by day and night they lie in ambush in the jungle, or on the plains near the roads, till they can pounce upon some unwary individual of the enemy. His murder is then communicated to his friends in a singular way. Forty or fifty Nagas, armed with wooden clubs, strike a large hollow piece of wood called a tomkhong, from which a loud, terrific sound proceeds, which gives token to the enemy that one of their tribe has died in acquittance of the debt of revenge. To such an extent does this vindictive spirit prevail, that the Nagas will wait for two or three generations devising plans for decapitating a member of a tribe who has murdered one of their clan; and when the opportunity of vengeance offers, they are sure to take advantage of it, regardless of the personal innocence of the man whom they select as the victim of their fury. The death of the victim is hailed with dance and song, and the liveliest demonstrations of joy: even the old men, women, and children seem in raptures at the announcement of the joyful tidings that their tribe has succeeded in taking revenge.

Naga Customs from Childhood until Marriage.

Ten days after the birth of a child the hair of the infant is shorn off, and the parents perform several ceremonies, inviting all their friends to a grand feast, on which occasion the child is named. On proceeding to field work the mother ties the child to her back, and whilst at work the infant is placed on the ground. When the child is about a year old it is left at home in the village, and the parents pursue their avocations unattended by their little charge. At the age of five or six years, some of the Nagas wear a lungtee (a small piece of cloth) round the waist. On attaining the age of nine or ten years the boy is called a Moorungea, and from that time no longer resides with his parents, but, with all the youths of the village, takes up his abode at the Moorung, a large building set apart for this especial purpose. The parents, however, still continue to provide him with food, and he is obedient to their will, assisting them in cultivating their fields. He carries a sword and spear, and wears the Naga habiliments. At fifteen or sixteen years of age he begins to be dissatisfied with his existence in the Moorung, and makes arrangements for taking a wife; generally selecting a cousin, the daughter of his mother's brother. On these occasions the parents collect as much rice and liquor, and as many cows and buffaloes, as their means will admit. The girls all live together, like the boys, in a separate Moorung or house allotted for them; sometimes they reside in a house in which a corpse is kept, probably from the greater sanctity such an inmate would confer on their habitation. The youth is not restricted from visiting the damsel of his choice, and he adopts a well understood stratagem to ascertain her sentiments regarding himself. Whilst he is talking to her companion, he carelessly puts down his pipe, and narrowly watches her actions. If the damsel entertains any regard for him she instantly takes up his pipe and smokes it; from that moment the youth is satisfied of his conquest, and hastens to communicate the result to his parents, who arrange matters with the girl's relatives. Presents of ornaments are sent for the girl, which she immediately wears; and an offering of liquor and tumbool pan (or betel nut leaf) to chew, being accepted by her parents, the marriage is decided on. After this, cows, buffaloes, rice, and liquor are forwarded to the house of the intended bride, and all her relations and friends are invited to a grand feast. An old Deodhunee (or priestess) accompanies the youth to the party with a basket of ginger, and the youth then addresses the chosen damsel, thus:—"This day I take you to be my wife. I will not desert you, neither will I take another; eat this ginger in pledge thereof—henceforth we are husband and wife." The woman on this eats a bit of the ginger, and then the youth sits down; whereupon the girl, in the same strain, taking up a piece of ginger, says—"I am your wife, and you are my husband, and I will obey you as such. I will not take another husband, for we are husband and wife; in token of which you will eat this ginger." The marriage ceremony being thus concluded, the youth, after partaking of the feast, returns home to his parents, and in the evening his wife joins him with baskets of food for her husband's parents and his brothers' wives. She thenceforth resides with her husband. From that day the husband ceases to abide at the Moorung, and after the lapse of two or three days, according to the village roll, takes his tour of guard duty at the Moorung. From the day of his marriage he commences the preparation of a separate house, upon the completion of which, in a few months, he quits the parental roof. Some Nagas will, however, continue to cultivate the land, and share the produce of their labour with those of their parents; but on the birth of a child the families separate.

Amongst the Nagas, marriage is contracted with near relatives, such as cousins, in preference to other women. A widow, having no children, cannot marry a stranger, but must marry her late husband's brother; and if he happens to be a mere boy, she will still live with him as his wife; nor can the boy take another damsel: he *must* marry his brother's widow. The custom is one of great antiquity, and apparently cannot be infringed. If the widow has one or two children she cannot marry again, but must remain in her own house. No Naga marries more than one wife, and if she dies he is at liberty to marry again.

The crimes of adultery and seduction are treated with the utmost severity: the offenders are brought before the Khonbao and the people assembled to investigate the offence; on proof of which, the Khonbao, or his Ticklah, decapitates the man in a conspicuous part of the road, between two or three villages; or he is tied with cane cords to a tree and there crucified. In some clans it is the practice to deprive both the seducer and seduced of their lives; in others, the former is placed in a basket, his hands and feet tied together, and he is rolled many times from the summit of a hill until life be extinct.

Funeral Ceremonies.

The Nagas consider sudden death as particularly unfortunate: even if a person dies after one or two months' sickness, the period is still deemed too short to be lucky; and his corpse is instantly removed and placed in the jungles on a platform four or five feet high, where it is left to decay. For three or four days after a death, the relatives do not leave the village; neither do other villagers resort to the village in which death has occurred during the same period. If a person dies who has been afflicted with a long illness, a platform is raised within his house, and the corpse being folded in clothes is placed thereon. By night and day the corpse is watched with great care, and as soon as it begins to decompose, large quantities of spirituous liquor are thrown over it; and whatever the deceased was in the habit of eating and drinking in his lifetime (such as rice, vegetables, and liquor) is placed once a month on the ground before the body. The virtues of the deceased are frequently rehearsed; the heirs and relatives throw themselves on the earth, and make great lamentations for many months after the death has occurred. At the expiration of the period of mourning, a great feast of liquor, rice, buffaloes' and cows' flesh is prepared by the survivors; and an immense number of people, armed with their swords and spears, and dressed in the most fantastical garb, as if preparing for a war expedition, are assembled to partake of it. They commence the festival by repeating the name of the deceased, singing many kinds of songs, dancing and cursing the deity or spirit in these words: "If to-day we could see you, we would with these swords and spears kill you. Yes, we would eat your flesh! yes, we would drink your blood! yes, we would burn your bones in the fire! You have slain our relative. Where have you fled to? Why did you kill our friend? Show yourself now, and we shall see what your strength is. Come quickly,—to-day, and we shall see you with our eyes, and with our swords cut you in pieces, and eat you raw. Let us see how sharp your sword is, and with it we will kill you. Look at our spears, see how sharp they are: with them we will spear you. Whither now art thou fled? Than thou, spirit, who destroyest our friends in our absence, we have no greater enemy. Where are you now?—whither hast thou fled?"

With these and similar speeches and songs, they clash their swords and weapons together, dance, and eat and drink throughout the night. On the following day the corpse is folded up in a cloth and placed on a new platform four or five feet high; and the whole of his weapons, swords, spears, panjees choonga (hollow bamboo joint, for holding water), rice-dish,—in fact everything used by the deceased in his lifetime, is now arranged round his bier, which is held sacred: no one would dare to touch a single thing thus consecrated. After this ceremony is concluded, the whole of the party disperse to their respective homes.

On the death of the Namsungea Khonbao, who, it is said, was one hundred and twenty years of age, his corpse was removed in December 1843, and according to an ancient custom, a tusk elephant was purchased from the Muttuck Bur Gohain, and killed, with three hundred buffaloes and pigs; when the Nagas enjoyed a magnificent feast. The usual practice of reviling the deity, while singing and dancing, was kept up with uncommon fervor, and the bacchanalian scene has perhaps seldom been exceeded. The heads of the slaughtered animals were suspended round the platform within a large enclosure, and the corpse was strewed over with an abundant supply of all kinds of forest flowers.

Naga mode of disposing of the dead on a Bier or Platform.

Theft is held in great abhorrence amongst the Nagas, and is consequently so rare that they leave everything exposed in the open fields. If any person is detected in committing the offence no mercy is shown: the Khonbao pronounces sentence of decapitation without a moment's hesitation. The Nagas are remarkable for simplicity, candour, and integrity; even the comparatively small vice of lying, to which the natives of British India are so seriously and universally addicted, is unknown among them, and will probably continue so until they have been corrupted by their more enlightened neighbours, the Assamese, or by the advance of civilization, refined arts, and manners. The Nagas have no names for the days of the week, and know not their own ages. Summer and winter are the only divisions of the year they recognise, distinguishing them as dry and wet seasons of six months' each. Time is counted by the moon, or by the number of crops they can recollect reaping. They believe in a God or Spirit called Rungkuttuck Rung, who created the earth and all things, but they have no hope of future rewards, nor any fear of punishment hereafter; neither do they believe in a future state of existence.

For the above information we are indebted to Bhog Chund, who is the son of a West Countryman of the Khetree caste, by an Assamese mother, and having lived many years amongst the Nagas, is thoroughly acquainted with them. He is now a resident and industrious cultivator in the plains. He reads and writes Assamese, and is a most straightforward character. He would be an invaluable companion and guide in travelling through the Naga territory.

I do not vouch for the correctness of the list of the Naga tribe inserted in a later page, but in the absence of more authentic details, it may be deemed worthy of consideration. The present account of the tribes is confined to the Nagas of Upper Assam; but it is supposed that very similar customs and habits prevail amongst those of central Assam. The Nagas bordering immediately on the plains are, for the most part, amicably disposed towards the British Government; and those on the Patkoe range have shown a desire for our protection against the marauding Singphoos. The Nagas residing on the hills most remote from the valley are said to be fine, stout, athletic men, of fair complexions; and unencumbered with the smallest strip of covering in the shape of clothing for any part of the body.

In 1842–43, the Namsangea, Bordoareah, and Borkhoormah Nagas invited a party of the Khetree to visit them as friends, but when they got them into their power they treacherously massacred twenty-four persons. Thageng, one of the Khetree party, being only wounded, fled and communicated the catastrophe to his tribe, who at the sight of his wounds prepared for revenge; and in a short time they were successful against the Nagas. The Khetrees, being ignorant of the Assamese language, were unable to pass through the territory of their enemies to report their grievances to the British authorities at Jeypoor. They accordingly went to Tomkhoomana, and lying in ambush, surprised and cut off the heads of twelve men of the Borkhoormah tribe, in revenge for the murdered of their own tribe. Upon this the civil authorities proceeded to the village of the Khetrees to endeavour to put a stop to these atrocious assassinations, but unfortunately the Namsangea and Bordoareah Nagas, contrary to strict injunctions, persisted in following in the wake of the British embassy of peace. The Khetrees perceiving the advance of their enemies, placed in the road a small basket of ginger kuchoos and a spear, as a token of submission to the British Government, but loudly protested from the summit of their hills against a visit being made to their village; dreading, as they did, the vengeance of the Namsangea and Bordoareah Nagas. The interpreter, Bhog Chund, who accompanied the party, entreated the Khetrees to remain quiet in their village, and to listen to terms of peace; but they indignantly rejected the offer, and threw down stones, and discharged a volley of spears, upon the advancing embassy. This being returned by a few rounds of musketry in self-defence, the Khetrees fled from their village to the neighbouring inaccessible hill fastnesses. The Namsangea and Bordoareah Nagas perceiving this, instantly rushed into the deserted village, slaughtered all the cows, pigs, and fowls, and burnt every house to the ground. After this untoward event a retreat was necessary, for the Khetrees came upon the party, throwing down stones and spears from their hills. A Sepahee having loitered in the rear, was speared to death, and his head and hands cut off and triumphantly stuck up on bamboos: the head in the village of Najoo, and the hands in Khoekting. After some difficulty the little detachment was extricated from its perilous position, and retreated in safety. Shortly after this lamentable affair, a larger military detachment was sent out; but to the present time an amicable settlement has been impracticable. Almost immediately after the last expedition, the Khetrees cut off the heads of eight men of the village of Bulatin; from which we may infer that their animosity continues unappeased, and that there is little hope of these savages being speedily brought to a sense of the advantages attending a reconciliation. Our intercession might be effectual for a time; but it is more than probable that it would be incompatible with a Naga's sense of honour to forego his greatest delight—revenge.

From the figured statement obtained from native authority, it would appear that there are one hundred and four Naga villages in Upper Assam, containing eleven thousand and ninety-five houses, with a population of forty-eight thousand five hundred and eighty-eight persons; but this estimate is probably erroneous. We shall perhaps be nearer the truth, if, assuming the number of houses to be correctly stated, we allow three persons for every dwelling: this gives a census of thirty-three thousand two hundred and eighty-five souls—a closer approximation to the apparent population.

List of the Naga Tribe.

No. of Villages.	Names of Villages.	No. of Houses.	No. of Persons.	Remarks.
1	Bur Dovar	250	1000	
2	Namsang	160	520	
3	Kea Mae	140	500	
4	Poolung	120	420	Three villages of this name
5	Panee Dooar	160	520	
6	Choongpon	140	500	

7	Khamgin	120	420	
8	Kokil	100	400	
9	Gophcha	70	280	
10	Topee	50	200	
11	Hungkal	80	320	
12	Dadum	250	1000	
13	Nerung	200	800	
14	Bako	300	1200	
15	Kekhyah	200	800	
16	Nahoah	180	720	
17	Nahoo	220	880	
18	Khoncha	50	200	
19	Lootong	50	200	
20	Kotong	70	280	
21	Nokphan	80	167	
22	Choupcha	120	480	
23	Choupnon	180	567	
24	Runow	200	800	
25	Rucha	60	140	
26	Changnee	220	880	
27	Changeha	160	567	
28	Pokum	80	167	
29	Loknean	80	167	
30	Changnoege	360	1340	
31	Changcha	120	480	
32	Mangnoe	120	480	
33	Mangcha	60	167	
34	Picktoo	80	320	
35	Pickta	55	220	
36	Nakma	70	200	
37	Moolong	90	263	
38	Bhetur Namsang	120	480	Entirely naked
39	Now Gawn	160	540	
40	Kangchang	100	415	
41	Dekahnoe Moong	140	520	
42	Borachaemoong	150	540	

43	Chamcha	60	180	
44	Achuringea	70	220	
45	Toormoong	120	480	
46	Jamee	100	400	
47	Moloo Thopea	500	4000	
48	Akhoea	270	2020	
49	Pocho	120	480	
50	Bor Langee	150	550	
51	Soro Langee	100	400	
52	Bhuga Langee	120	480	
53	Chenajow	150	560	
54	Boora Gaea	150	550	
55	Bur Dorea	150	540	
56	Kula Barea	200	800	
57	Soroo Durea1	20	470	

Nagas east of the Namsang River subject to the Political Agent, Upper Assam.

No. of Villages.	Names of Villages.	No. of Houses.	No. of Persons.	Remarks.
1	Khetree Gawn	110	440	
2	Khena	80	180	
3	Bottin	60	120	
4	Namcha	70	140	
5	Mooktong	90	240	
6	Hakhoom	80	280	
7	Konagaun	150	550	
8	Khatung	40	190	
9	Jankung	60	420	
10	Ken Noean	50	200	
11	Naktung	60	240	
12	Lalrung	60	240	
13	Koonum	80	330	
14	Kootung	70	340	
15	Mooaloo	120	480	
16	Moacha	80	320	

17	Tejhon	80	280	
18	Chomjoo	90	320	
19	Somcha	60	240	
20	Kambao	100	400	
21	Langchang	100	400	
22	Sooroomungchang	60	240	
23	Noanangchang	50	200	
24	Tikhak	50	200	
25	Gudie	60	240	
26	Manbao	110	440	
27	Eahung	110	400	
28	Mookkhoop	110	400	
29	Mookpe	120	480	
30	Mookcha	90	360	
31	Loongke	100	400	
32	Namnie	220	880	On or near the Pat-koe range.
33	Namcha	130	520	
34	Keme, No. 1	120	440	ditto.
35	Keme, No. 2	120	480	ditto.
36	Kintoonie	100	400	ditto.
37	Mookrung	120	480	
38	Joopee	50	200	
39	Doedam	70	280	
40	Noakhoorma	50	200	
41	Chobang	50	200	
42	Chilim	40	160	
43	Bachowuk	50	200	
44	Moung	60	240	
45	Hadoot	80	260	
46	Kaeah	90	300	
47	Kaejou	110	440	
	Total	3,000	15,398	
	Total of Statement No. 1	8,095	33,190	
	Grand Total	11,095	48,588	

GARROWS.

The Garrows: the tallest and most powerful of all the hill tribes—Savage custom on the death of their relatives—Description of the Garrow women—Culture of cotton—climate

Of all the hill tribes bordering on the Assam valley, north or south, the Garrows near Goalparah, though not lofty in stature, are endowed with the most powerful herculean frames. The expression of their countenances is savage, and their complexion exceedingly black. In conversation they are loud, and remarkable for asperity. Passing through Lookee Dooar to the Jeypore stockade, at the foot of the Garrow hills, I met with many Garrows who reside on the low hills bordering Assam, and learned that they were frequently in great danger from the highland Garrows; who, feeling secure in their mountain fastnesses, made occasional incursions into the territory of the former, and committed acts of violence upon the British subjects located in the plains.

A savage custom exists amongst the Garrows, of commemorating the death of their relatives by massacring our inoffensive subjects whenever they can do so with impunity; whether in open day, in ambush, or by a sudden night attack in overwhelming numbers. In this respect they resemble other tribes of which we have already treated. At their festive meetings it is said the Garrows are guilty of great excesses in imbibing spirituous liquors. A dried excavated gourd, which does duty for a bottle, and holds about one quart and a half, is filled with an intoxicating liquor distilled from rice: this, at their jovial parties, is presented to each person, whose nose being seized, the gourd is applied to the mouth till the individual is perfectly satiated, or falls prostrate in a fit of intoxication. After this, the toper is immersed in a pool of water, or the river, that the temperature of the body may be cooled. In the choice of food few things come amiss to a Garrow palate. For example, a dog fed with rice and then roasted alive, is esteemed one of the most exquisite dainties. Every description of meat is consumed, even when perfectly putrid. Singularly enough, however, milk is considered unwholesome, and is never drank.

The Garrow women are remarkably coarse and ugly, with very dark complexions. They wear scarcely any articles of cloth covering, but, in common with most savages, they are particularly fond of showy ornaments. Their necks are adorned with a profusion of coloured glass beads; and if the lobe of the ear can only be distended to the shoulders by the weight of ear-rings, they consider that they have succeeded in rendering themselves peculiarly attractive. The Garrows to this day are independent of our rule, and are, therefore, free from any tax on their cultivation.

An immense quantity of cotton is grown on their hills. This, until 1843, was subject to a tax paid by the purchaser to Government, at the market, where the Garrows bring down their cotton for sale; but, owing to the mal-practices of the native collectors appointed to receive the customs, little profit accrued to Government after the expenses of the establishment had been paid. For the encouragement of trade and a freer intercourse with our people, the customs have lately been entirely abolished; but it is supposed that a plan for the assessment of the whole of the Garrow cultivation will, if possible, shortly be adopted. The climate of the Garrow hills, however, offers a serious obstacle to this measure; for, according to our present information, no European constitution could endure a lengthened residence amongst them; and without the constant presence of a British officer, armed with authority to arrange their affairs, neither the advancement of civilization, nor the realization of a revenue sufficient to defray the expense of retaining and settling the country, could be accomplished. It is supposed that a lac of rupees, or ten thousand pounds sterling, might annually be raised from the land; but our knowledge of the country and the resources of the people is so limited, that this estimate cannot be relied on. Moreover, from the known aversion of the Garrows to any sort of taxation, the undertaking can only be rendered successful by the presence of a large body of British troops; to whom the sword, spear, and poisoned arrows of the savages could offer but little effectual resistance.

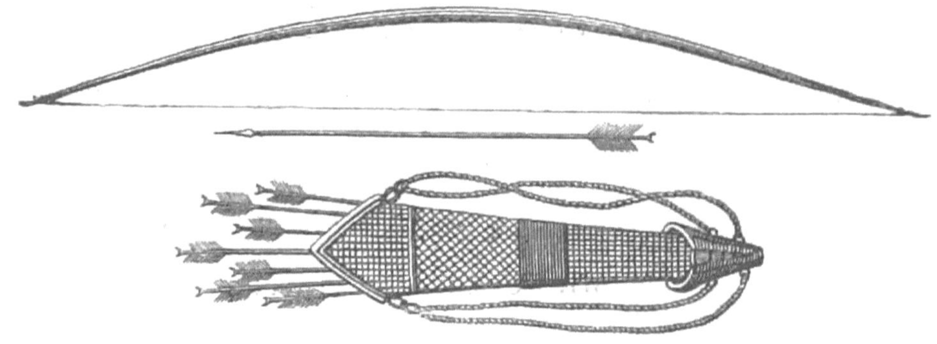

Garrow Bow and Arrows.

COSSEAHS.

The Cosseahs: An athletic race, but indolent—Murder of Lieuts. Beddingfield and Burlton—Chief product, potatoes

This tribe, although near neighbours of the Garrows, are unlike them in personal appearance. They are an athletic race, but by no means fond of more occupation than will suffice to give them a bare subsistence. This gained, their lives are passed in fishing, bird catching, and hunting, merely by way of pastime. Like all savages, they are untrustworthy.

In the year 1829 at Nuncklow, Lieutenants Beddingfield and Burlton were, by the Cosseah Rajah's order, barbarously massacred. A regular war ensued; consequent on which Rajah Teeruth Singh was deprived of the district of Bur Dooar, and the Rajah of Pantam having joined the Cosseahs, his district was also sequestrated. At this period, no protecting force being at hand, the Garrows joined the Cosseahs and invaded the districts of Bur Dooar and Pantam, accompanied by the people, who were compelled to join the insurrection. The movement, however, was quickly suppressed by military detachments. Since then the Cosseahs have been vigilantly watched by the Sylhet Light Infantry, stationed at Chirrapoonjie.

In the Cosseah hills a large supply of potatoes is annually raised and sold in the Gowahatty market, realizing to the Cosseahs no inconsiderable profit. The effect of this traffic being to promote a more frequent intercourse with the people of the plains, it is hoped that in course of time the Cosseahs may learn the value of peaceable commercial pursuits, and become a prosperous and civilized race.

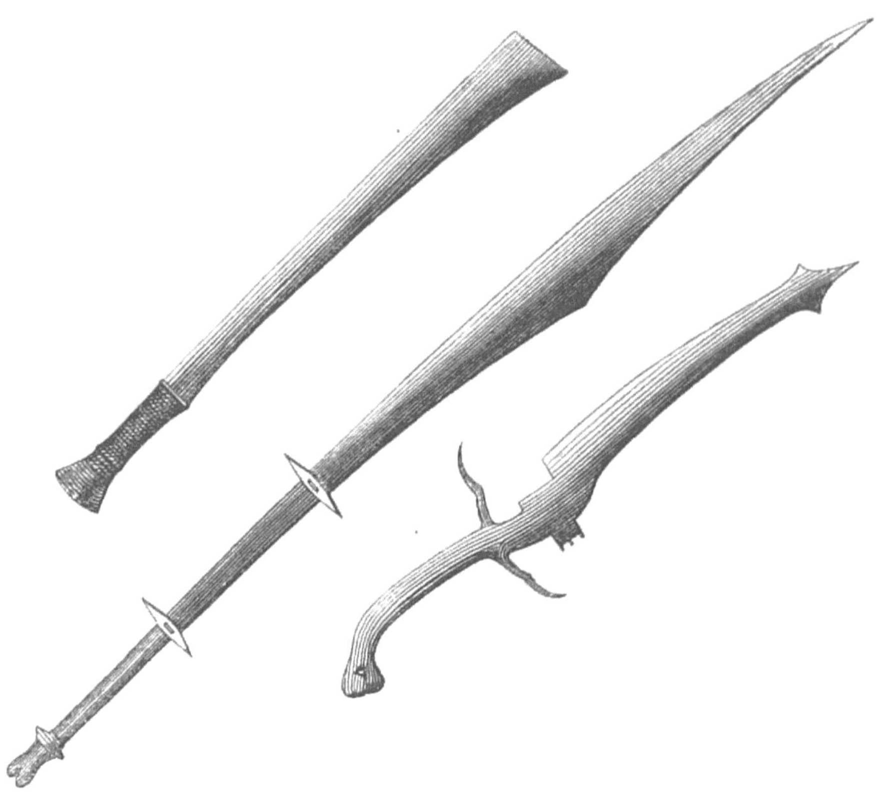

Singphoo, Cosseah, and Garrow swords.

BOOTEAHS.

THE BOOTEAHS: extent of the Bootan hills—Population—Captain Pemberton's description of the Booteahs—Exactions and malpractices of the Bootan rulers—Weapons

The hills of Bootan, about two hundred and twenty miles long by ninety broad, form the northern boundary of Assam. The population of the country, including the Dooars, is assumed at 145,200 souls, the Bootan hills 79,200, and the Dooars or low lands at 66,000; but this calculation, made by the late Captain Pemberton, has been proved to be greatly in excess of the truth, as regards the population of the Dooars. In 1842 a census was taken of five Dooars: namely, Ghurkola, Banska, Chapagorie, Chapakhamar, and Bijnee, in the Kamroop district; when it appeared there were about 10,000 inhabitants, and the net revenue of the tracts amounted to 17,544 rupees 7 ans. 4 pice, or 1,754*l.* 8*s.* 11*d.* It may, therefore, justly be inferred that the population of the whole of the Dooars would not exceed 40,000 souls. Captain Pemberton, the British Envoy deputed to Bootan in 1838, describes the Booteah to be "in disposition naturally excellent; he possesses an equanimity of temper almost bordering on apathy, and he is seldom sufficiently roused to give vent to his feelings in any exclamations of pleasure or surprise; on the other hand, they are indolent to an extreme degree, totally wanting in energy, illiterate, immoral, and victims of the most unqualified superstition. The punishment of the most heinous offences may be evaded by the payment of a fine, which for murder varies from eighty to two hundred Deba rupees, or 40 to 100 Company's rupees, or from 4*l.* to 10*l.*"

Polyandry, or plurality of husbands, prevails throughout Thibet and the northern parts of Bootan; and on the death of the head of a family his property becomes escheated to the Deba or Dhurma Rajahs, without the slightest reference to the distress entailed on the afflicted survivors. "The highest officers of state in Bootan are shameless beggars, liars of the first magnitude, whose most solemnly pledged words are violated without the slightest hesitation; who enter into engagements which they have not the most distant intention of fulfilling; who play the bully and sycophant with equal readiness, and are apparently totally void of gratitude, exhibiting in their conduct a rare compound of official pride and presumption with the low cunning of needy mediocrity; and yet preserving, at the same time, a mild deportment, and speaking generally in a remarkably low tone of voice."

Amongst the officers of the Deba or Dhurma Rajahs of Bootan, not one appears to have been entitled to the confidence of the Envoy. The habits of all classes are most disgustingly filthy, and in the mode of preparing their food little attention is paid to cleanliness, and still less to the quality of the meat they consume. On festive occasions they imbibe large draughts of the liquor called chong, which is procured by fermentation from rice. "The diet of the great body of the people is restricted to the refuse of wretched crops of unripe wheat and barley, and their food consists generally of cakes made from these grains very imperfectly ground; but the food of the Government officers and priests consists of the flesh of goats, swine, cattle, and rice, imported from the Dooars." The Dooars are large tracts of country leading up to the passes into the Bootan mountains. In January, 1842, they were all appropriated by our Government as a permanent measure; in consequence of the non-payment of tribute by the Booteahs, their "repeated acts of aggression in the murder and seizure of British subjects, and likewise for assisting to organize bands of robbers and sharing in the profits of their plunder." Whether the Bootan hills will furnish a sufficient support for their scanty population seems problematical; and if pressed by hunger it is not improbable the Booteahs will rush down and ravage the fertile plains of Assam. The measure was, however, indispensably necessary to prevent the frequent recurrence of oppression and systematic plunder of the people located at the foot of the Bootan mountains. The extensive territory denominated Dooars has always belonged to the Assam kings, and the Booteahs invariably paid tribute for the same. Their exactions and malpractices having imposed on the Government the necessity of depriving the Booteahs of a charge they were unworthy of retaining, this cannot be viewed as a harsh proceeding: it was most reluctantly adopted, and only when it became evident that the finest land in Assam had been converted into a desolate waste, overgrown with jungle and nearly depopulated, owing to the arbitrary severity of the Bootan rulers.

In December, 1842, a friendly meeting took place at Banska Dooar between the highest officers of the Bootan Government and the Governor-General's Agent. The Booteahs were attended by about two hundred followers; and during their few days' stay their complaints were fully entertained, and will probably be satisfied by the grant of a small annual sum as compensation for the loss they have sustained in the annexation of the Dooars to Assam.

During the interview the Booteahs were plentifully supplied with swine, the most acceptable gifts that can be offered to a Booteah; and an officer who was present on the occasion assured me that the incessant squeaking of the pigs, when roasting alive by these heartless barbarians, was most distressing, and the sight of the culinary process excessively disgusting. As soon as the animals had been partially roasted they were cut up, and, without any further preparation, re-toasted and speedily consumed.

The Booteah is a large, athletic man, of a dark complexion, with an unpleasant, heavy, but cunning countenance. Compared with other hill tribes in their neighbourhood, they are deficient in spirit and bravery. For example, in March 1836, A.D., a party of seventy-five Assam Sebundy Sipahees proceeded against six hundred Booteahs, who were posted in five masses, with a few men extended between each, at Soobunkatta, in Banska Dooar. When the Dewangerie Rajah was requested to retire with his troops; they answered the requisition with shouts of defiance and a simultaneous advance. Lieut. Matthews, perceiving the critical situation in which his little band was placed, instantly advanced to the contest, and, firing a volley and then gallantly charging with the bayonet, caused the immediate dispersion of the whole force, leaving on the field twenty-five killed and fifty wounded. The Dewangerie Rajah himself was closely pursued, and only escaped through the swiftness of the elephant on which he was mounted; his tent, baggage, robes of state, and standards, fell into the hands of the victorious Sebundies.

This trial of strength with our disciplined troops has taught the Booteahs to pay more respect to our power; and they are not likely to have recourse to arms again, unless greatly distressed for provisions, or urged by vain arrogance to imagine that a show of resistance may conduce to our resigning the Dooars to their rule.

A Booteah servant.

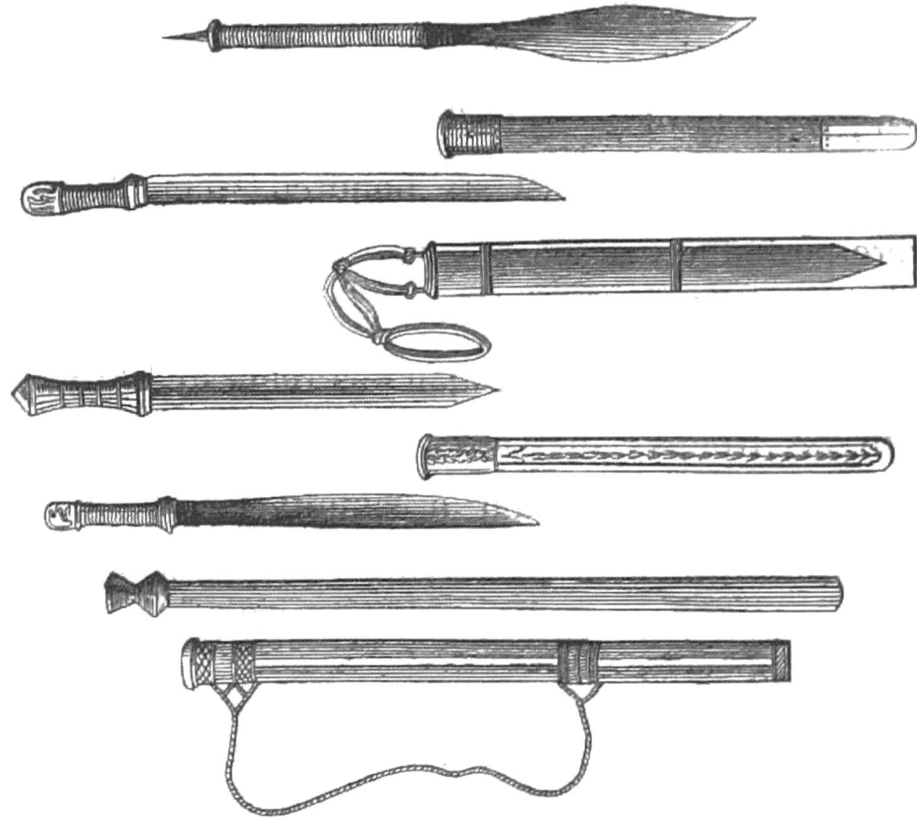

Booteah Weapons.

SATH BOOTEAH RAJAHS OF KOOREAHPARAH DOOAH, IN DURRUNG.

THE SATH BOOTEAH RAJAHS OF KOOREAHPARAH DOOAR IN DURRUNG: the mountains where located—Kalling and Booree Goorma Dooars—Tyranny of the Booteahs towards the Dooars—Kalling Dooar annexed to Assam—Kooreahparah Dooar—Exactions of the Sath Rajahs—Advantages of British Government

Having given a brief outline of the Booteahs of Banska Dooar in Kamroop, we propose now to detail a few authenticated facts and incidents connected with the remaining tribes noted above; who are located in the northern mountains between the Bur Nuddee west and the Kochoojan east, bordering on the Luckimpore district, north of the Burrampooter river.

And first commencing from the Bur Nuddee west, we find the Kalling and Booree Goorma Dooars belonged, for eight months in the year, to the Booteahs subject to the Tongso Pilo, under the Deba and Dhurma Rajahs of Bootan; during which time they levied upon the people contributions, or black mail, in the shape of rice, Erea cloths, and cattle. During the remaining portion of the year, from the 15th of June to the 15th of October, the people of the Dooars reverted to the jurisdiction of the British Government; and for the protection granted to them they paid an annual revenue, at a certain rate per plough. A hearth tax was likewise realized. But this double rule was attended with the most disastrous results. No man under the tyrannical Booteah Government dared evince signs of affluence, or even of comfort: the people were compelled, for their self-preservation, to dress in the miserable garb of the lowest Hindoo peasantry; for the mere suspicion of a person being possessed of any wealth, entailed on him the strictest espionage, and not unfrequently the seizure of the whole of his property. Not satisfied with this, if the slightest idea were entertained that there was money or other valuable property concealed (for it is the custom of the Assamese to bury their wealth underground), torture was resorted to without the slightest compunction, until the unfortunate sufferer confessed to having a hoard, and surrendered the little savings of a whole life to his merciless persecutors.

Such was the condition of the inhabitants of the Dooars till 1838: hundreds annually retreated to the Pergunnahs (districts) of Assam under British rule, to enjoy the fruit of their labours in peace and safety. The beautiful, fertile Dooars were then rapidly reverting to a barren wilderness: fearful exactions and cruel oppressions rendering the existence of the few remaining communities precarious and unendurable; until an unlooked for incident occurred to deliver the people from the thraldom of their demi-savage rulers. Gumbhur Wuzeer having long been suspected by the Booteahs of disaffection towards them, and of possessing great wealth, the Tongso Pilo of Bootan, through the Soobah Rajah, gave orders for his destruction; and in December, 1838, he was barbarously murdered. The whole of his property, amounting to 50,000 rupees, was confiscated, and his wives, children, and adherents, in all twelve persons, were carried away into the hills.

This outrage justly aroused the British Government to redress the grievances of a long oppressed people. The Dooar was immediately attached to Assam; and the Booteahs have never, to this day, sought pecuniary compensation for the loss of their territory. The son of the late Gumbheer Wuzeer was permitted to return to Assam in 1844, and resume the fiscal charge of his father's villages; and ere long, probably, the Booteahs of this tract will see the folly of their past conduct, and be glad to accept such compensation as the Government may be disposed to make them for the privation of their power to levy black mail from the people. The annual tribute realized from Kalling Dooar previous to its annexation, amounted to 390 rupees, and was collected in the following articles:—

	Rupees.
5 ponies valued at 60 rupees each	300
5 tolas weight of gold, at 12 rupees per tola	60
4 pods of musk, at 3 rupees each	12
4 cows' tails, at 1 rupee	4
4 blankets at 3 rupees each	12
4 daggers, at 8 annas each	2
Total rs.	390

From Booree Gooma Dooar the tribute of 232 rs. 10 ans. 8 pice was also paid in kind, viz:—

	Rupees.
3 ponies, at 6 rupees each	180
3 tolas of gold	36
2 pods of musk	6
2 cows' tails	2
2 blankets	6
2 daggers	1
Bags	1

At the present day the net revenue of Kalling Dooar amounts to 2080 rs. 0 ans. 4 pice, with a population of 1634 persons. Booree Gooma Dooar is estimated to contain 7785 souls, with a net revenue of 5348 rs. 5 ans. 3 pice.

Proceeding eastwards from Booree Gooma Dooar, the next Dooar, called

Kooreahparah, is under the Sath Booteah Rajahs of Naregooma, subject to the Towung Rajah, who is a tributary of the Deba and Dhurma Rajahs of Lassah.

Cheringtanjing. Gelae.

Booteah Rajah. *Booteah Rajah.*

Booteah Rajahs.

The country of Towung being in Kumpa or Thibet, quite distinct from Bootan, south of the Sampoo river, it appears that a portion of the Thibet territory, or more properly the Chinese and British frontiers, are actually in immediate contact in the Kooreahparah Dooar, about twenty miles from the Burrampooter river. This Dooar, as we have said, was governed by these chiefs eight months in every year. During this period, the seven Rajahs paid periodical visits to the Dooar, and let loose many hundreds of their followers to range throughout the Dooars, and quarter themselves gratuitously upon the people: changing from house to house until they had consumed all the food the poor Ryots had to give them. The Sath Rajahs had usually a caravan of large herds of ponies, mules, &c., as far as Umerathal, one march from Oodalgorie. On their arrival there, the inhabitants of the Dooar were compelled to take care of the cattle, and be in constant attendance on the Rajahs, furnishing them with supplies of rice, cloths, spirits, pigs, &c.; and at the approach of the hot months, the ponies, mules, and donkeys were laden with the whole of the collections levied from the people of the Dooar, and the chiefs retreated to the mountains at Nareegooma.

Such was the annual visitation to which the people were subjected the moment the four months of British rule expired. A gradual decrease of the population of the Dooar was the natural result of this tyranny; but the grasping oppression of the Booteahs underwent no diminution. They made no remission on account of the decay of the population: the same amount of collections was still drawn from the remaining Ryots. The country became overgrown with jungle, and the malaria of these plains was so injurious to the constitutions of Bengalees or Europeans, that the tract could not be visited with impunity for above a few weeks in the year. The fevers were most fatal, and life was frequently extinguished in four or five days. Thieves, highway robbers, and murderers here sought and found a safe asylum under the shadow of Booteah rule, by administering to the rapacity of the chiefs. They surrendered a portion of their ill-gotten wealth in the shape of fines for the protection given them, in opposition to treaties and the laws of civilized nations.

Such was the state of affairs, when, to the unspeakable delight of the inhabitants, the Dooar was attached by the British Government in 1839. A police thannah was established at Oodalgorie, British law was enforced, marauders and disturbers of society were quickly suppressed, and at the present day a prosperous population has again sprung up; only too thankful that they can enjoy the produce of the land in peace and safety, under a powerful Government capable of protecting them from the aggressions and exactions of the wild mountaineers. The contributions taken in kind from each house by the Booteahs consisted of five pieces of Moonjah silk, sar cloth, one piece of Erea cloth, one gumcha or handkerchief, Moonjah thread, and metal bracelets, worth altogether about one rupee and a half. Such, at least, was the estimate made by the late Mr. David Scott, the Agent to the Governor-General. But there can be no doubt that the Booteahs were in the habit of exacting as much as possible from the most wealthy in the Dooar, though from the poorest peasant they might have collected their black mail upon some settled principle. In this manner the sum annually collected would vary; but we have reason to believe that 5,499 rs. 15 ans. was the average sum levied on the Ryots in the shape of contributions in kind, and 411 rs. 13 ans. in black mail or ready cash.

The Booteahs, it is affirmed, yearly brought down presents of various articles, such as salt, blankets, &c., which they gave to the Ryots. These presents were valued at 966 rs. 15 ans., which being deducted from the supposed amount of the value of the contributions above noticed, the Sath Rajahs, it would appear, received 4944 rs. 13 ans. Upon this data, in 1844, a permanent settlement was made with these chiefs. They agreed to resign all claim or title to collect black mail in the said Dooar for the future, on condition of receiving 5000 rs. from the British Government as compensation for the sacrifice they made. The tribute paid in kind from this Dooar, previous to its attachment in 1839, amounted to 397rs. 8 ans., namely:—

	Rs.	*Ans.*
4 ponies at 60 rs. each	240	0
5 pucka tolahs of gold	60	0
4 kucha tolahs	40	0
3 pods of musk	9	0
Cows' tails	3	0
9 blankets	27	0
Bags	2	8
3 red striped Erea cloths	3	0
Honey	3	12
Contingencies for the care of the ponies	7	8

The principal persons who subscribed to the treaty of February, 1844, at Tezpore, were Sanjiee, chief of the Sath Rajahs, Sering, Tangjing, Changdundoo, and two Bramee agents from the Towung Rajah. The latter had no credentials empowering them to execute any deed or to agree to any particular terms; but, as the Towung Rajah had never deigned to reply to the communications hitherto made to him, the apparent informality was deemed of no consequence; and, from the very liberal terms proposed, no difficulty was experienced in effecting so desirable a settlement.

The population of the Dooar is estimated to be 22,577 persons, and the net revenue 12,455 rs. 7 ans.

CHAR DOOAR, OR SHEERGAWN AND ROOPRAE BOOTEAH SATH RAJAHS.

THE CHAR DOOAR, OR SHEERGAWN AND ROOPRAE BOOTEAH SATH RAJAHS: names of the principal chiefs—Yearly amount of black mail levied by them—Murder of Moodhoo Sykeah

The appellation of Sath Rajahs, or Seven Chiefs, appears to be commonly in vogue amongst the Booteahs; but we have yet to learn the origin of its adoption, as the number of chiefs, both in the Kooreahparah and Char Dooars, is by no means confined to seven. The Sath Rajahs of the Char Dooar levied black mail from the people precisely in the same manner as their brethren in the Kooreahparah Dooar. The principal chiefs are the Durjee Rajah Tangpoor, Jyphoo, Dakpah, Sankandoo Sangjaa of Roopre, Chang Wangdundoo, son of the late Rajah Tangjung of Sheergawn. They reside at Sheergawn and Rooprae, about three days' journey from Dymara pass, by which they descend into Char Dooar. They are quite distinct from the Booteahs of Kooreahparah Dooar, and do not admit that they are subordinate to the Towung Rajah.

These chiefs, until 1839, yearly realised 2526 rs. 7 ans. black mail, exclusive of 416 rs. 8 ans. which was deducted for collecting the contributions from the Ryots in the shape of food, clothing, &c.; but in April, 1839, Moodhoo Sykeah, the Patyhery of Ooorung, having been barbarously murdered by some Booteahs of the above-named clan, they were from that date a proscribed tribe, and prevented from deriving any benefit from the Dooar in collecting black mail. Refusing to give up the murderers, all access to the Dooars was strictly denied them, and they were justly regarded as unworthy of any consideration. They frequently denied having any authority over the murderers, pleaded the hardship of the whole body being made to suffer for the faults of a few individuals, and expressed their extreme regret at having incurred the displeasure of the British Government.

Moodhoo Sykeah's fate is supposed to have arisen from his attachment to the British Government, and the energy displayed by him in causing the land to be measured, to effect a regular assessment thereof, in lieu of a plough and capitation tax. Such an arrangement was particularly repugnant to the Booteahs, as they imagined it would interfere with the Ryots paying them their black mail; they therefore took vengeance on the promoters of this measure, and Moodhoo Sykeah was cruelly cut to pieces in his own house by Booteahs partaking of his hospitality. Gumbheer Wuzeer had been similarly treated the year before, under suspicion of too great an attachment to the British Government, and a desire to carry out their views. In 1844 the chiefs were permitted to visit Tezpore, and in consideration of the contrition evinced by them, and the uncertainty as to whether the murderers were still in existence, and really belonged to that tribe, Government was pleased to overlook the past, and again to receive them into favour. In lieu of all right or title to collect black mail, compensation to the amount of 1740 rupees per annum was settled upon them.

THEBINGEAH BOOTEAHS.

THE THEBINGEAH BOOTEAHS: quarrel between them and the Rooprae Booteahs of Char Dooar—At the present day not numerous, but peaceable and inoffensive—Sum allowed them by the British Government in lieu of black mail

Of all the tribes of Booteahs inhabiting the interior or most northern mountains, the Thebingeahs appear to be the most easterly. About forty years ago a quarrel arose between them and the Rooprae Booteahs of Char Dooar, regarding the right to collect contributions or black mail from certain Bohoteahs, or slaves. Being defeated, the Thebingeahs were for eleven years denied all access to the plains by their unrelenting foes. Previous to this feud, the former had the right to collect the whole of the Booteah dues from Majbat; but after this, their black mail was appropriated by their opponents.

Having, about twenty-nine years ago, partially made up matters with their enemies, the Rooprae Booteahs, the Thebingeahs again visited Assam, and have since that time made collections in Majbat in conjunction with them. Formerly, as they aver, they were the channel through which the Char Dooar Booteahs sent tribute to Towung. Before the quarrel, their route to Assam lay through the Char Dooar Booteahs' country; but since then it has been abandoned, and they now enter by that of Kooreahparah Dooar. At the present day their numbers are very small, and they appear to be a peaceable, inoffensive race.

The town of Tibbung is stated to be sixteen days' journey from the plains of Assam. For the first twelve days the route lies through the country belonging to the Kooreahparah Booteahs. The next march brings the Thebingeah Booteahs to their own frontier village of Sangtie. The Thebingeahs are tributary to the Towung Rajah, who is subordinate to the Deba and Dhurma Rajahs of Lassah. In speaking of Lassah, they make the distance from their country much greater than there is reason to believe it to be. They aver that in going to Lassah they cross a great river (probably the Sampoo) which is the Lohit or Burrampooter, that traverses the whole valley of Assam. Towung is said to be twenty days' journey from Tibbung, in a westerly direction. From the little information we have hitherto been able to gather, it is evident the Thebingeah Booteahs were once a powerful tribe; but feuds and exterminating wars with other neighbouring tribes have reduced them to an insignificant state. The British Government generously bestows on this clan 141 rs. 13 ans. 6 pice per annum, in lieu of the black mail they formerly extorted from the Ryots of the village of Majbat in Char Dooar.

HUZAREE KHAWA AKHAS.

The Huzaree Khawa Akhas: reside in the mountains north of Burgong—Formerly very powerful, but now acknowledge the supremacy of Taggee, a Kuppah Choor Akha Chief

These tribes reside eastward of the Rooprae and Sheergawn Booteahs, in the mountains north of Burgong, called the Jumara Guyah hills, distant from Burgong, viâ the Dymarahhat or market, about six difficult marches. The whole of the Akha tribe is reported to consist of two hundred families; the Kuppah Choor Akhas, of sixty or seventy families; and the Meeches (who are also, like the Kuppah Choor Akhas, a tribe of Akhas residing far in the interior, north of the whole) are estimated at three or four hundred families. The whole are armed with bows and arrows, and long swords, but they have no fire-arms of any kind. The Huzaree Khawa Akhas were formerly the most formidable of the two clans, but through the energy and daring of Kuppah Choor Akha chief, Taggee, they have been obliged to acknowledge him supreme. His will at the present day may be said to be paramount; for though his contemporary chiefs profess to look on him as their friend and equal they fear to incur his resentment, and submit to his dictation with concealed feelings of dissatisfaction.

Previous to the massacre of a detachment of the 1st Assam Light Infantry at Baleeparah, the Huzaree Khawa Akhas had always collected Pocha or black mail to the yearly amount of 175 rupees; but after the above catastrophe they were looked on as outlaws, and were denied all intercourse with the people of the plains. In February, 1844, however, the following chiefs of this tribe were summoned to Tezpore, and an annual sum of 148 rupees was settled upon them; on the condition of their abstaining from committing further depredations on our subjects or joining with other disaffected tribes:—

		Rs.
Nizam Rajah		60
Changja		32
Changtoang		32
Kebelon		24
	Rs.	148

KUPPAH CHOOR AKHAS.

The Kuppah Choor Akhas: always looked upon by their neighbours as a ferocious band of banditti—Depredations by Rajah Taggee—His incarceration by the British, and subsequent liberation—Resorts to his former lawless practices—Massacre of the Goorkha Sipahees—Taggee, in 1842, voluntarily surrenders to the British, who again liberate him on his swearing allegiance—He is pensioned with four other chiefs

From all the information obtainable regarding this tribe, they appear to have been always looked upon by their neighbours, the Booteahs and Dufflahs, as a ferocious band of Dacoits or banditti, living entirely upon plunder, and never scrupling to shed blood for the successful prosecution of any unprovoked aggressions, whether on the Booteahs, Dufflahs, or British subjects. In this light the late Mr. David Scott, Agent to the Governor-General, on his first visit to the Char Dooar, regarded this clan. Considering that they had no right or title to collect pocha, or black mail, he verbally directed that they should be treated as enemies, and not allowed to enter the British territory: if they attempted it, the guards were to fire upon them. This was absolutely necessary; as the Taggee Rajah, just prior to our conquest of Assam, and during the Burmese government, had frequently committed serious depredations on the people; and on one occasion he ransacked several villages, and attacked the estate of Pond Borowa of Char Dooar, who was barbarously murdered with twenty-five of his followers. In 1829, the Taggee Rajah and his Kuppah Choor Akhas had a quarrel with the Akhas of Somgsong Rajah. Many lives were lost in the prosecution of this feud, and the Taggee Rajah was at last obliged to take refuge at Burgong, in Char Dooar. Brijnath Hazaree had the courage instantly to apprehend him at Gorahgong; and, putting him in irons, sent him down to Mr. D. Scott, then at Gowahatty. Here he was incarcerated in the common gaol for four years; at the expiration of which period (in 1832–33) Mr. Robertson, the then Agent to the Governor-General, directed his release and allowed him to return to his native hills, in the hope that this act of clemency would secure his future fidelity and attachment to the British Government. But Mr. Robertson was deceived. No sooner did this child of the forest and the mountain find himself again at liberty, than, regardless of his engagements, he immediately collected together a few of his old followers, and, by the mere influence of his savage character, he soon rendered himself independent of the Towung Rajah, and took tribute from the Rooprae and Sheergawn Booteahs. He then resorted to his former lawless practices of rapine and destruction; declaring that, now he was released from the Gowahatty gaol, he would not rest until he had sacrificed every man who had aided in apprehending him. Such was the terror his name inspired, that the slightest report of his approach alarmed the inhabitants of the plains, and they deserted their villages in the utmost consternation. It was well known that no quarter was given or mercy shown by the freebooter: men, women, and children were indiscriminately butchered; neither life nor property was respected; and safety was only attainable by timely flight.

Cheegee Kuppachor Akha. *Brother of the Tagee Rajah.* Kuppachor Akha. *Tagee Rajah.*

Kuppah Choor Akhas.

At one time it was the practice in Assam to locate small bodies of troops in stockades along the frontier, north and south of the valley at the foot of the hills; or in the immediate vicinity of hostile tribes, so as to overawe them and prevent predatory incursions into our plains for the capture of slaves and plunder. These posts, being far distant from the support of the head quarters of the respective regiments, and away from the immediate control of European officers, discipline and vigilance were perhaps too little regarded; and the consequence was, that detachments were not unfrequently surprised and massacred in the most savage manner. In 1835, there was a stockade at Baleeparah in Char Dooar, garrisoned by one havildar, one naick, and six sipahees of the 1st Assam Light Infantry. About 10 o'clock A.M. of the 3rd of February of the same year, the Kuppah Choor and Akha chiefs, Taggee, Nizam, and Somgsong, accompanied by a few daring followers, proceeded to the stockade: the havildar, unsuspicious of any treachery, went outside to converse with the Taggee Rajah, and told him that he must not enter the stockade. After a short conversation the Taggee Rajah—as a signal understood by the Akhas, drew his sword and inflicted a wound on the havildar's left leg. Nazim Rajah then cut down the Naick with his own hand, and the whole of the Akhas instantly rushed on the havildar, entered the stockade, and murdered every person they could seize; slaughtering in all sixteen persons: the havildar, naick and four sipahees, and the wives and families of the Goorkha sipahees. Two sipahees of the guard happened to be bathing in a tank close by at the time of the attack, and saved their lives by running into the jungles. After the massacre, the Taggee Rajah set fire to all the houses inside the stockade, and retired with his followers to the fastnesses in the neighbouring hills.

Intelligence of this disaster reaching the civil authorities, a proclamation was immediately issued, offering a reward of five hundred rupees to any person who would bring the Taggee Rajah, dead or alive, and two hundred rupees for any information that would lead to his apprehension. This proclamation, however, was in 1837–38 modified by the express order of the Honourable Court of Directors, who intimated that the proceeding was most exceptionable, and that rewards should only be given for the apprehension of offenders, and not for slaying them. From that day until 1842, the whole tribe of Akhas and Kuppah Choor Akhas were treated as outlaws. Our outposts were strengthened, and all British subjects prohibited from furnishing them with grain or any other necessaries of life.

In 1842, the Taggee Rajah, of his own free will, came down from the hills and surrendered himself to the British Government. The excuse pleaded by him for the massacre of the guard was the tyranny and insolence of the sipahees towards his tribe; but it does not appear that the sipahees had any quarrel with the Akhas or Kuppah Choor Akhas, and it is therefore reasonable to conclude that the latter destroyed the guard because they were posted there to prevent depredations on the plains. Notwithstanding the crimes committed by the Taggee Rajah, Government directed his release, on his swearing future allegiance on his own behalf and that of his tribe. This was a matter of necessity: there were no means at hand of summarily punishing the outrage that had been committed, and the influence of the Rajah was requisite to curb the future irregularities of his people. As an inducement to him to restrain a rapacious banditti from future aggressions, a pension of twenty rupees per mensem was bestowed upon him for life. The Taggee Rajah, it might have been supposed, returned to his native hills somewhat appeased and gratified; but here again the British authorities were erroneous in their calculations. Incapable of comprehending our motives, and distrustful of our purposes, the Rajah, for two years, never resorted to the station of Tezpore to receive his pension. In 1844, however, an interview with himself and other chiefs took place, and an amicable and satisfactory arrangement was made. The Taggee Rajah received his pension of 240 rupees per annum granted in 1842; Nechoo received 24 rupees; Sankhandoo, 32 rupees; Seerkoolee, 32 rupees; Sorsoo, 32 rupees: in all five chiefs, their pensions amounting to 360 rupees per annum.

Thus terminated a desultory, harassing war of twenty years with one of the most restless tribes on the frontier. The manner in which the forbearance of these savages has been purchased will, we are persuaded, not be misconstrued into fear or weakness, but be productive of future peace and security and a freer intercourse with the people of the plains.

DUFFLAHS.

The Dufflahs: Divided into innumerable clans—Very uncivilized, and formerly very troublesome—In 1836–37, consent to forego their depredations on receiving a fixed sum from the British Government—List of Dufflah chiefs, and the amount of pension paid to them

The Dufflah tribes are divided into innumerable petty clans, and reside in Char Dooar, Now Dooar, and Chuh Dooar. They are a very uncivilized race of beings, and formerly were extremely troublesome: committing atrocities, attacking and kidnapping the people of the plains, and extorting a large amount of black mail in kind annually. To enumerate the several petty robberies, disturbances, and murders committed at different times by these wild mountaineers, would, at the present day, be neither interesting nor profitable: it will suffice to remark that the people are all disunited, living under independent chiefs with separate interests, and have never leagued together in large bodies to ravage the plains for plunder or the capture of slaves. No union seems to prevail amongst them as with the Singphoos, Abors, and Khamtees; their irruptions and depredations, therefore, are always on a small scale. Almost every clan seems suspicious of its neighbour, and the sanguinary feuds amongst themselves are frequent. Of their religion, manners, customs, and habits, we regret to say little is known, and that little of a character not to be relied on: the same may be said of our information respecting the Akha tribes.

In 1836–37, an agreement was entered into with the Dufflahs to forego their extortions on receiving from the British Government a fixed sum in lieu of all demands. Unlike the Booteahs, who cannot live in the plains, the Dufflahs seem disposed to adopt agricultural habits; and considerable numbers have deserted their hills and located themselves in the plains, paying revenue for the land they cultivate at the same rate as our Ryots. From these symptoms of industry, we are led to hope that in the course of time others will follow their example, and descend from their hills to enjoy the protection of the British Government; when their condition will be greatly ameliorated.

A Dufflah. A Dufflah Chief's Widow. A Dufflah Chief.

Dufflahs.

In Char Dooar there are no less than one hundred and eighty Dufflah chiefs, belonging to twelve distinct clans, who receive 1,020 rupees per annum in lieu of the black mail formerly extorted from the Ryots. In the Now Dooar, there are nine dooars (passes or tracts of country leading into the northern hills) occupied by fifty-eight Dufflah chiefs, who receive compensation or a pension from Government of 1,523 rupees 9 ans. annually in lieu of black mail; making a grand total for both Dooars of 2,543 rupees 9 ans. 8 pice. It remains only to notice the amount supposed to have been collected as black mail by the Dufflahs from the people in Now Dooar previous to the year 1836–37, when a pecuniary compensation was given to the Dufflahs in lieu of this objectionable exaction. The contributions levied as black mail were nearly all given in kind. On the arrival of the Dufflahs once a year, from their mountains in the Now Dooar, it was their custom to take from the Sahoorea Ryots Government free pykes (or men), from each house:—

	Rs.	*Ans.*	*Pice.*
1 seer of salt, valued at	0	4	0
5 seers of rice	0	1	0
Ready cash	0	1	0
	0	6	0

and if the ready money of one anna was not paid, a Moonga, or Erea Gumcha, or handkerchief valued at three annas was taken instead. On their return to the hills, another cess or contribution, amounting to 7 rs. 10 ans. was levied from each village or community, fixed originally at twenty houses; and whether they had decreased or increased in numbers the Dufflahs neither reduced nor augmented their demand. The articles taken from each village consisted on this occasion generally of—

	Rs.	*Ans.*	*Pice.*
1 Erea cloth, valued at	3	0	0
1 Moonga Gumcha handkerchief	0	4	0
1 cow	2	8	0
Cash, as a present	1	0	0
Rice, 1 bhar	0	4	0
1 duck	0	2	0
1 seer of salt	0	4	0
1 seer of oil	0	4	0
	7	10	0

Besides the Sahoorea, or free population, there were four villages (Baghmarra, Bihalle, Sakomata, Bakola) wholly inhabited by Cacharees, who were denominated Bohoteahs, or slaves; being free men bestowed originally by the Assam kings for a particular purpose or service. This caste or tribe the Dufflahs especially considered as their slaves, from whom they claimed the right to collect two-thirds of the produce of their labours. Each Bohoteah received from the British Government two poorahs of land, and one rupee only was taken from him as revenue, or capitation tax; being two rupees less than that paid by the Government Pykes. The remission of two rupees granted in his favour, was to enable him to meet the demands of the Dufflahs against him, in addition to the following amount of black mail, viz:—

	Rs.	*Ans.*	*Pice.*
1 Erea small cloth	1	0	0
1 Moonga gumcha	0	4	0
1 chunam (or lime box)	0	8	0
1 kuttaree, or knife	0	2	0
1 jappee hat or umbrella	0	4	0
1 bhar of rice	0	4	0
1 duck	0	2	0
1 seer of salt	0	4	0
1 seer of oil	0	4	0
	3	0	0

From this it would appear that the Bohoteahs paid to the Dufflahs five rupees each in produce; while the free population was assessed at the rate of about eight rupees per village of twenty houses, which would average about six annas four pice per house. From the free and slave population united, as far as we have means for determining, the sum realized in kind from the inhabitants of the whole Dooar, amounted to 2,503 rs. 10 ans. 6 pice; so that in reality the Dufflahs have gained by the money substituted for black mail.

In the palmy days of the Ahoom Government it is not certain that this system existed; but on the Ahoom Rajahs becoming proselytes to the Hindoo creed, they and their followers degenerated; and being unable to check by force of arms, the inroads of the numerous hill tribes both on the north and south frontiers of the valley—a space of 400 miles, accessible by innumerable passes—they readily permitted the tribes to levy black mail once a year on certain portions of land called Dooars. Thus were continual hostilities averted, and the Ahoom Rajahs had leisure to pay attention to their own affairs. Intestine commotion, however, worked the destruction which foreign aggression was restrained from accomplishing.

Char Dooar Dufflahs.

No. of Chiefs in each Khel or Clan.	No. of Khels or lans.	Name of Khel or Clan.	Amount of Pension.		
			Rs.	*Ans.*	*Pice.*
23	1	Phering Ooela	97	8	5

20	2	Oopur Takoolea	108	5	2
21	3	Nam Takoolea	196	14	1
21	4	Rapo Oolea	76	11	4
46	5	Paee Olea	234	12	2
7	6	Oopur Taolea	17	1	11
2	7	Nam Taolea	3	10	7
3	8	Chana Oolea	23	6	7
37	9	Oopur Tabungolea	106	2	9
	10	Purbutea village, Mekla Gaum, Deka and Bur Gaum extinct	4	8	4
	11	Jeynath Hya Babang Gaum, of Kuchla Barru, extinct	0	8	3
	12	Names of chiefs unknown, extinct	150	0	0
180		Total	1020	0	0

Dufflahs Of Now Dooar.

No. of Dooars.	Name of Dooars.	No. of Chiefs	Name of Chiefs	Amount of Pension		
				Rs.	*Ans.*	*Pice.*
1	Bihalee Dooar.	1	Tamoo Gaum			
		2	Tetae			
		3	Ruma			
		4	Nerbow			
		5	Tumes			
		6	Emakolee Gaumnee			
		7	Hollee Gaum			
		8	Hathemorea Huraporah	58	9	7
2	Gong Dooar.	1	Bhoot Gaum			
		2	Ruma and Gamoo			
		3	Akho Chalee Gaumnee			
		4	Changdur Gaum			
		5	Rao			
		6	Nizboo and Burkmal			
		7	Rungoa and his son Byragee	82	2	8

3	Bagmara Dooar.	1	Gopee Gaum			
		2	Papoong and Kadoo			
		3	Sedae Gaum			
		4	Teeta Gaum			
		5	Lalloo			
		6	Kowa			
		7	Baboo			
		8	Madoo and Paree	29	5	11
4	Sakhoo Mata Dooar.	1	Deka Gaum, Bogle, and Rumgka			
		2	Chale Gaema, Gotoa Gaum			
		3	Kena Gaum	262	8	5
5	Chooteah Dooar.	1	Babung Gaum			
		2	Bengala Gaum			
		3	Bengakoe Gaum			
		4	Chengolee Gaum			
		5	Hanoo Gaum			
		6	Tadung Gaum			
		7	Hanoo Gaum			
		8	Peroo Gaum			
		9	Durpur Gaum			
		10	Taggee for Talee			
		11	Teloa Gaum			
		12	Tamar			
		13	Durrung	234	0	3
6	Kuchlahbaree Dooar.	1	Phedula, Bhedo Jey, Nizae Bulae Jey Gaums			
		2	Ladoom			
		3	Onee			
		4	Rungoma			
		5	Tajur	66	1	3
7	Chandhur Dooar.	1	Jeyram Gaum			

		2	Ketula Haree			
		3	Bogee Gaum			
		4	Hetoo Gaumnee	137	12	8
8	Gurea Dooar.	1	Beroo Gaum, Seram Nirboo Keah Gaum			
		2	Dhunae Darkeh	46	11	10
9	Bakula Dooar.	1	Neema Gaum			
		2	Gobind Gaum			
		3	Peroo Gaum			
		4	Tama, Jagura, Nerum Lekejoo Luchoo, Begora, Oozeer, and others			
		5	Chengalee and others			
		6	Khakung Gaum			
		7	Halee			
		8	Chedar	606	5	1
			Total paid to Now Dooar, Dufflah Chiefs	1523	9	8
			Total paid to Char Dooar Dufflah Chiefs	1020	0	0
		58	Total	2543	9	8

9 789361 383922

Printed by Libri Plureos GmbH in Hamburg,
Germany